MW01244587

PRAISE FOR
PATIENT CARE THE SANDLER WAY

"A must read for any healthcare enterprise that truly cares about sustainable growth."

—**BRENDEN SCHULTEK,** Director,
U.S. Field Sales, QuVa Pharma

"There have been so many changes in the healthcare field that it has become difficult for physicians and medical practices to remain competitive while avoiding the risk of burnout. I would recommend this book to all healthcare providers aiming to succeed in this turbulent market. Donna outlines how medical professionals can use the core Sandler principles to grow their practices."

—**SUSAN SEGAT,** Owner,
Strategic Marketing Systems

"We operate in an increasingly complex environment. Fortunately, this book offers some very simple and effective principles for transforming the patient experience. It works so well that I brought Donna and the Sandler approach with me when I changed positions and moved to a new practice!"

—**LAURA WHINFIELD,** Marketing Director,
Esana Medspa & Plastic Surgery Center

PATIENT CARE
THE SANDLER WAY

PATIENT CARE
THE SANDLER WAY

*Running a Great Medical Practice
That Has Patients Cheering and Staff Engaged*

DONNA BAK

Sandler Training

Paperback ISBN: 978-0-692-83856-3

E-book ISBN: 978-0-692-83857-0

To Team Bak

Michael, Alexander, and Emily

You're the best thing that ever happened to me.

To my parents

Richard and Joyce

You're the most wonderful parents I could have ever asked for.

CONTENTS

ACKNOWLEDGMENTS

Writing a book has been a dream of mine ever since I can remember. I have the following individuals to thank for helping make my dream come true.

To the healthcare professionals with whom I've had the honor of working: You change lives every day, and you certainly changed mine. Thank you for the gifts of empathy, compassion, and a healthy dose of good humor.

To my Sandler® colleagues around the world: You inspire me to go way outside my comfort zone—to move beyond what's familiar and into what's possible.

To everyone at Sandler's home office: Your fingerprints are all over this book, and I'm grateful for each of you.

To Laura Matthews and Jerry Dorris: Your editing and layout work made all the difference to polish and refine this book.

To my editor, Yusuf Toropov: You have helped me to become a better reader, writer, and trainer. It was a privilege and a pleasure for me to work with you on this book.

To David Mattson: You gave me the opportunity and then the resources to make my dream come true.

To my team at PEAK Sales Performance: Thank you for your encouragement. To Ed Schultek especially: Your friendship has changed my life profoundly. Thank you for helping me to dream big.

Writer Stephen King is often asked what his secret for success is, and he attributes it to staying physically healthy and staying married. Staying physically (and mentally!) healthy is hard work. Staying married is easy when you're married to the greatest guy in the world. You're the secret to our success, Mike. Let's grow old and stay healthy together.

FOREWORD

It's hard to think of a segment of the economy that has had to deal with more turbulence, public scrutiny, and controversy in recent years than the healthcare sector. Yet even with all the media coverage, all the drama, and all the high-profile disagreements, one persistent reality has consistently remained under-examined: Patients expect a better level of service—and many of them are ready, willing, and able to change providers if doing so means receiving a better in-person experience.

Here's the good news. Healthcare professionals have more control than they may imagine over the quality of both the patient experience—and, by extension, over their own level of satisfaction in the workplace. Donna Bak's new book shows how to reclaim this control. It leverages classic Sandler Selling System® communication principles and adapts them to the healthcare environment, allowing professionals to transform the dynamic of their interactions with patients—and with each other.

Patient Care the Sandler Way is a long-overdue contribution to the essential, ongoing conversation about improving both the quality and the sustainability of the healthcare experience.

David Mattson
President/CEO, Sandler Training

INTRODUCTION

The Big Question

> *The greater danger for most of us lies not in setting*
> *our aim too high and falling short; but in setting*
> *our aim too low, and achieving our mark.*
> *—Michelangelo*

I s your practice a great practice?

Great medical practices look and sound different than their competition. Sure, profitability contributes to greatness, as does superior medical expertise—but these are not enough.

Great medical practices also put a high priority on delivering an extraordinary experience—for both their patients and their internal staff. In doing so, they are better positioned to withstand the pressures and demands that naturally occur in the medical field. They are less vulnerable to external forces and stronger internally. Healthcare professionals at great medical practices experience less stress on the job and treat each other with more respect.

> *Inevitably, a question arises for every medical practice:*
> *"Are we good—or are we great?"*

A good medical practice focuses on production levels in the hopes of making a profit. If enough patients come through the practice in a day (the theory goes), the practice will be profitable. Along the way, though, there are a lot of challenges: complex payment processes, government regulations, hassles with insurance companies, the need to see more and more patients, high staff turnover, difficult people and situations, and, last but not least, a deepening sense that the patient experience is not what it should be.

A great medical practice faces all of the same challenges except for the last one. It manages to transcend the challenges by focusing on: profitability, medical expertise, and creating a positive experience. This experience is so positive that patients can't stop talking about it. Patients talk to friends, relatives, and acquaintances about the care they received. They can't help posting nice things about this great practice on social media. They can't imagine recommending anyone else.

As you can see, this model is a little different than that of the merely good medical practice. If enough patients come through the practice in a day, stay with the practice year after year, and rave about their positive experience to their family and friends, the practice will grow in patients and health scores will rise.

There's more. In a great medical practice, healthcare professionals treat each other as equal peers, and they treat each other with respect. They elevate themselves to perform at a higher level. They don't want to work anywhere else.

Does your practice put a high priority on creating an experience that leaves patients thinking, "Wow!"? Is customer care an ongoing conversation, not a one-time event? Do you have a work environment in which colleagues treat each other as internal customers? Or is profitability and medical expertise the only focus of your day?

THE SANDLER PATIENT-CARE TRAINING APPROACH

This book will give you a detailed overview of Sandler's approach to patient-care training. This approach has been implemented successfully by medical practices in a variety of disciplines. Each of these practices has taken team performance to the next level. Healthcare professionals are given the opportunity to master the "inner game" that creates and sustains a respectful, productive, low-stress environment for both patients and staff.

In Sandler's Patient-Care Training Approach, healthcare professionals learn:

- How to develop proven skills to deliver an exceptional experience that leaves patients and peers smiling.
- How to approach their job with positive attitudes and productive behaviors that transform the way they think about themselves, their peers, and their patients.

Sandler Training provides long-term and incremental reinforcement training and coaching to ensure a significant, lasting return on the training investment. We not only help your medical practice bridge the gap between where you are today and where you want to be in the future, but we get you there sooner. This book is only the beginning. Read it, and then let's continue the discussion.

HOW GOOD IS
YOUR SLINGSHOT?

CHAPTER 1

The Beginning

> *Never look back unless you are planning to go that way. —Henry David Thoreau*

M y client Dr. George Upward (not his real name) realized he was playing David to someone else's Goliath on a chilly Monday morning when he accidently left the dining room window open.

George, a general practitioner doctor, was serving as CEO of Upward Medicine, a multi-office practice in Oregon City, Oregon. He liked to come downstairs at home to read the morning paper before starting his day. George was a traditionalist who read the local paper in print form, turning physical pages of newsprint while he sipped his coffee. As he consulted the *Oregon City Eagle*, though, his blood ran cold. Even when he got up and shut the window, the cold feeling inside wouldn't leave him alone.

There on the back page of the first section was a full-page ad for his competitor MajorCareWest, touting the high quality of their patient care. Of course, the big hospitals and specialized care centers had huge media campaigns behind them—campaigns that dominated social media discussions. George knew his practice couldn't afford that. He didn't plan to compete that way. But what on earth was one of his own patients—or, come to think of it, a former patient—doing in MajorCareWest's ad giving such a glowing recommendation?

George grumbled and flung the paper onto the table. He took a long pull of black coffee, then set the cup down. JoAnne (not her real name, either) had been a patient of his some time ago. George's day had gotten off to a bad start.

He picked up the latest issue of *Oregon Medicine*, the trade

> *"They've got everything they need to deliver a perfect patient experience, every single time. I love MajorCareWest and can't imagine going anywhere else!"* —JoAnne Choices

magazine to which he subscribed, and started flipping through the pages to get his mind off the ad he'd just seen. But the very same ad, with the same endorsement, showed up on page five.

"I give up," he said, louder than he'd meant to. "I cannot believe this."

"Give up on what?" called his wife Marie from upstairs.

"Nothing!"

She apparently believed him. "Honey, I have an appointment at Northwest Chiropractic at 9:00. Can you drop me there on your way to work? I have a friend picking me up when I'm done."

"I suppose."

"You suppose?"

"Yes. Yes, I can. Yes."

"OK—thanks."

What mystified George was how other practices in Oregon City—chiropractors, dentists, pediatricians—somehow rang up all those love letters. Take Northwest Chiropractic, for instance. Just last night, some of its patients had posted a wave of positive messages on Northwest's Facebook page. George pulled up the page on his phone and read it once again. As he did, he shook his head.

"The people at Northwest are the best! They treat you like a human being. Cannot recommend them highly enough."

"My mother-in-law recommended this chiropractic office to me. So glad she did. Wonderful place. Check them out."

"It's like my whole life turned around after the folks at Northwest got to work on my back. Pains I had been used to living with for years disappeared literally overnight. Go see these people!"

What is up with these posts? George thought. *Are they for real? Or does Northwest have an army of paid endorsers, posting away online or something? Wait a minute—* George squinted at the ad and got a real jolt. That last one was from his wife Marie! *What is going on here?*

George had been worrying for weeks that his practice might be vulnerable to a merger with a competitor, and those splashy full-page ads hadn't done anything to calm his fears. He knew he wouldn't be able to compete against a combination of profitability and exceptional care. As his practice's patient flow slowed down—and patient turnover increased—he was already under a lot of pressure. The last thing he wanted to do was to be acquired by another practice.

As he drove Marie to her appointment, he started thinking about what it would be like to work for MajorCareWest. He didn't like that option much: the shame of defeat; the loss of autonomy; the frustration of not having a seat at the decision-making table.

"You missed the exit, George."

"Sorry. Sorry, dear."

CHAPTER 2

The Competitive Challenge in Healthcare

> I tell the kids, somebody's gotta win, and somebody's gotta lose. Just don't fight about it. Just try to get better. —Yogi Berra

My client George is not alone.

Leaders in the healthcare profession come to Sandler for different reasons, but they usually share with us one or more of these concerns:

- They are unsure of how to keep a productive flow of patients coming through the practice without hurting the patient experience—and ultimately, compromising the practice's future.

- They feel pressured by patient demands for better service. Patients know they have choices. Staff is losing motivation. A-players are leaving. Doing nothing about it is not an option anymore.
- They struggle with sounding different from their competition, leaving them with no point of difference—and vulnerable to mergers and acquisitions.

There are often other concerns as well: stagnant or shrinking market share, flat growth, changes in reimbursement models, increases in malpractice insurance, and a dwindling flow of new patients. Issues like these have always been threats to the success of a medical practice. But the inability to compete against the larger medical practices or hospitals—the Goliaths in healthcare—is new for many practices, and some are better at this than others.

DAVID AND GOLIATH, THE HEALTHCARE VERSION

The story of David and Goliath tells of the young shepherd boy David who volunteers to fight the giant Goliath. Goliath is armed with a massive club at the end of his tree-trunk–sized arm. Knowing that he can't possibly compete against Goliath's strength, David chooses instead to use his skill with a slingshot. In the story, he defeats the formidable Goliath with a single well-aimed stone.

So the question for you and your practice is: How good is your slingshot?

Offering your patients the best medical technology and medical expertise isn't enough anymore. For medical practices to thrive in today's competitive market, they need a slingshot—a point of difference—to win and to keep winning. That point of distinction isn't a new piece of equipment, or a new alliance with another practice, or a spiffy new marketing campaign. There is nothing wrong with any of those things in and of themselves. They're just not a slingshot.

In order to survive and compete successfully in today's market, you must deliver a *wow!* patient experience that turns patients into what authors Ken Blanchard and Sheldon Bowles call "raving fans." (In fact, *Raving Fans* is the title of their book.)

Raving fans are not the same as satisfied patients. Satisfied patients are the ones who tell you, after a visit, that they were generally happy with the level of care they received. Raving fans, on the other hand, would go out of their way to choose you again over a competitor, would not replace you with a competitor under any circumstances, and would enthusiastically recommend you to friends and family who are foolish enough to think of going elsewhere.

Most medical practices do not have raving fans. If they're lucky, they have satisfied patients. (Not many, truth be told, are even that lucky.)

How do you build a practice that generates such responses from patients? How, in other words, do you build a slingshot?

CHAPTER 3

Why Conventional Approaches Don't Work

> *Life begins at the end of your comfort zone.*
> *—Neale Donald Walsch*

I f you were to ask George from Chapter 1 whether he'd trained his team well enough to generate "raving fan" responses, he would have replied, "Of course I have. We've spent a lot of time training our people in patient care."

He'd have been correct, at least about that last part. George has indeed invested time, effort, and energy in various patient-care training regimens. The trouble is the typical customer or patient-care training simply doesn't work in healthcare.

George was skeptical about this when he first came to Sandler for help. He thought of patient-care training for his staff as something you checked off a list, preferably over the course of an hour or so, but if necessary over the course of a weekend. Then, you didn't bother with it again, ever—until you had a new hire. But a big part of George's skepticism lay in his misunderstanding of what patient-care training really is.

WHAT HOLDS PEOPLE BACK

In every job, there are tasks and behaviors that employees are good at, comfortable with, and enjoy doing. These are the tasks that are always at the top of their to-do list. The tasks and behaviors that come to them naturally are right within their comfort zone. There are also tasks and behaviors in the job that make employees uncomfortable, which they avoid by rationalizing why they can't do them. These are the tasks that often are left over on a to-do list at the end of the day. They are the tasks and behaviors employees shy away from—not because they can't do

> *Conventional patient-care training typically doesn't address how to keep employees from drifting back to their old behavior—the tasks and behaviors they're most familiar with, their comfort zone—once the training is over.*

them, but because they're not comfortable doing them. These tasks and behaviors and habits are outside their comfort zone.

There's nothing out of the ordinary about having a comfort zone, and there's nothing bad about not feeling like stepping out of it. That's the human condition. Yes, it's a little scary when people must take on a new behavior that lies outside of what they're familiar with doing. But the fact that it's a little scary doesn't mean they shouldn't do it. Wasn't it a little scary when you learned to ride a bike? Wasn't it a little scary the first time you tried to parallel park? Wasn't it a little scary when you paid the rent or mortgage on your own place for the very first time? Wasn't it a little scary the first time you drew blood from a patient or gave someone an injection? Yet imagine a world where you never learned to ride a two-wheeler, where you were doomed to search the city forever for a head-in parking place, where you never set up house on your own, where you were never able to give a patient who needed one an injection.

David Sandler, the founder of Sandler Training, used to say that, in the situations that really matter, you only have to be brave for five seconds at a time. He was absolutely right. Human beings are wired to be able to challenge their own comfort zones and grow as a result of that challenge. Humans wouldn't have survived as a species otherwise. Sometimes individuals can lose sight of that, but it's true. You're actually happier and more fulfilled when you're growing and challenging yourself.

You can probably think of a few things in your job right now that make you feel nervous, embarrassed, self-conscious, anxious, or maybe even inadequate. Maybe it's addressing conflict, or doing something for the first time, or speaking in front of a group, or selling your services, or taking a stand on something when it goes against the majority, or advocating for yourself, or failing—and on and on. Healthcare professionals, including doctors, often feel uncomfortable bringing up any time-related issues with patients. For example, the doctor is running late, there are no available appointments for several weeks, the doctor (usually for valid reasons) has to rush through appointments, or the patient may not get a call back about a question within 24 hours. Dealing effectively with time—too much or too little of it—is outside the comfort zone of many healthcare professionals.

If you're like most people, you will look hard for, and usually find, all kinds of creative ways to avoid doing things outside your comfort zone. But consider this. What if you were able to get beyond your discomfort and perform these uncomfortable tasks or behaviors for just long enough to create a breakthrough? Would you overcome a fear that you know is holding you back both personally and professionally? Let's pretend for a minute that you could overcome this fear. Would you have a better quality of work—heck, a better quality of life?

HOW DID YOU LEARN TO RIDE A BIKE?

Training that doesn't push you beyond your comfort zone, training without reinforcement over time, won't work—not when it comes to creating sustainable, productive new behavior patterns.

Once upon a time, you didn't know how to ride a bicycle. Now, I'm guessing, you do. How did that happen? It was easy enough not to ride a bike. In fact, you were pretty good at not riding a bike. Then you saw the kids around the neighborhood riding around on their bikes. It seemed like something you ought to be doing. You got some coaching from a friend, parent, or sibling. The first time you tried to pedal without training wheels was a little scary. Your coach helped you through that. You took a deep breath. You pedaled anyway. You fell down. You got back up. Your coach talked you through it. You fell down. You got back up. Your coach talked you through it. You repeated that process.

It didn't happen overnight. But, thanks to ongoing reinforcement, it did happen. At first, riding without your training wheels was well outside your comfort zone—right? Then at some point you moved to a point where riding a bike was inside your comfort zone. Maybe then one of the kids you played with started popping wheelies, and you had something new to expand your comfort zone around (after listening to a boring lecture from your parents about bike safety, of course).

This experience of learning something new by expanding your comfort zone is universal—which is why we talk about it as much as we do in all of Sandler's training programs. We emphasize it because it is the "secret sauce" that leads to personal and organizational success in just about any field of endeavor—including patient care.

I realize you may have heard something like this before. There is a secret sauce for most everything in life, from losing weight to finding love to attracting and keeping patients, and everything in between. Lots of books promise to tell you how to accomplish these kinds of things, and lots of experts claim to have the ingredients to the secret sauce that will enable you to have a breakthrough in their chosen area of expertise.

Although most of the sauces people write books about should work, the truth is they don't. Why not? Because they don't provide a strategy for overcoming the discomfort inherent in doing new behaviors that will take you outside your comfort zone. That's what George's previous training programs didn't have: a strategy for overcoming the natural inclination to stick with the familiar that most adults develop by the time they are about 30 years old.

Adult learners do best with a regimen of ongoing reinforcement with trainer and peer support over time. The Sandler approach uses that regimen to challenge you to feel the discomfort, do it anyway, and notice what happens.

> *A medical practice will not get a return on its training investment unless the people are being trained to move outside their comfort zone and perform at a higher level.*

This is what George didn't take into account. It doesn't matter how good the patient-care curriculum is or how good the trainers are in delivering the material. It's the shift from comfortable to uncomfortable—from mediocre to exceptional—that's at the heart of the Sandler Training® approach. This is why our clients get a strong, rapid return on their training. In other words, you can't teach someone to ride a bike by showing him a video of a bike-riding kid. He has to be hands-on, and you've got to coach.

MOVING BEYOND THE FAMILIAR

George the CEO was used to getting through his day in a certain way. He had built up a certain momentum, a certain force of habit, when it came to dealing with questions related to the patient experience. Complaints from patients? Bad reviews online? His solution was to point people toward those posters they handed out during customer-care training. That's what lay inside George's comfort zone. It wasn't getting him or his practice where he wanted to go.

Not only that, the doctors in his practice were also used

getting through their day in a certain way. They, too, had grown accustomed to how the staff interacted with patients and with each other. If they were truthful with themselves, they'd agree that the patient care was usually mediocre and the staff interactions were good, not great. They would say things like, "It's a problem of commitment," or, "The staff members aren't doing their job," or, "It will pass." No matter how often they repeated those mantras, though, the communication problems didn't seem to go away. To the contrary, they seemed to be getting worse.

In fact, everyone in George's medical practice—all the people who worked with the patients—were used to doing things in a certain way, too. They'd say things like, "No one understands how hard we work," or, "I just smile, do what I'm told, and get through the day," or, "Why all this fuss over patient care when we're so busy?" These mantras, too, didn't seem to be improving the situation.

> *Every employee of a practice lives in a world in which everything they do and say connects with what the customer experiences. That means, instead of repeating mantras or stories, they need to change their perspective and ask some new—and braver—questions.*

WHERE THE MAGIC HAPPENS

In order for any sustainable positive change to occur at Upward Medicine, in order to move the patient experience from "about what you'd expect" to "I have got to tell people what a great practice this is," George, like each and every member of the team, had to answer this question:

"Why should I bother going outside my comfort zone?"

Seriously, why bother with behavioral change? Why bother with reinforcement? Why bother disrupting mediocrity?

Different people within the practice are going to have different answers to that question.

For executives like George, the answer to the question, "Why should I do something different?," lay in the increasingly competitive healthcare marketplace itself. He didn't want his practice to be merged or acquired by a larger competitor. Years ago, George had made a conscious choice not to go work for a hospital. He would have had fewer day-to-day worries if he'd made the decision the other way because (let's face it) a hospital takes care of everything He could have shown up for work each day and just practiced medicine, letting the hospital executives handle all the decisions about what building to use, how to pay for it, what equipment to secure, how to pay for that, who to hire, who to fire, how to retain key staff, when and how to expand the practice, and so on. But that's not what George wanted. He had more of an entrepreneurial spirit. He wanted to chart his own destiny. Self-determination was a big issue for him. He wanted to maintain control of the practice and grow it over time.

So for George, doing something different meant there was an opportunity to reduce these stressors:

- He'd reduce his worry that the business would no longer be able to stay autonomous and independent.

- He'd reduce his concern that the team would not be able to perform at peak levels and thus would not increase patient load or achieve the efficiencies necessary to hit agreed-upon performance targets.

- He'd reduce his anxiety over whether the business would end up facing malpractice suits from hostile or dissatisfied patients or paying higher malpractice insurance premiums.

For one of the doctors on George's staff, Raina Rapport, MD, the answer to the question, "Why should I do something different?," was pride.

Her concerns took the following forms:

- Worry that the level of team cohesion was dropping steadily—and would continue to drop after she retired, which she anticipated doing in a few years.

- Concern that the legacy she left behind at the practice would not be one that reflected her years of service or experience.

- Discomfort with the quality of communication in the workplace.
- Anxieties that matched or exceeded George's about the possibility of increased malpractice liability.

Raina wanted to walk away from a practice that operated the way it had when she first signed on in the vastly different economic environment of a few decades earlier. The medical world then was more patient-centered, it was easier to generate recommendations, and the environment was more supportive of both patients and employees. That wasn't what she saw when she showed up for work now, and that troubled her. She was also bothered by some of the interpersonal challenges she witnessed (and experienced) during a typical day in the practice. She knew there had to be a better way for the team to get through the day.

Raina had helped to found the practice. In her view, the early days of the practice—back when she had been the only physician doing clinical work—were stronger in terms of patient care, and she wanted to leave a legacy of superior service at Upward. She wanted to put the practice's name on the map in terms of patient care. "How cool would it be," she asked her team one morning, "to be known as the practice that does it differently, the practice that has the patient in mind, the practice that delivers a *wow!* experience?"

For Raina, how the patient is treated was a critical issue. She wanted to leave her fingerprints on this part of the practice. She wanted to raise the standard of the patient experience—not just for a week or a month, but for long after she retired. She had a feeling that transforming how people within the practice treated each other was going to be a big part of that.

What about the people in charge of supporting the doctors, notably Ellen Everywhere, who worked the majority of her hours at the front desk? If you're a healthcare professional like Ellen, you may be wondering right about now the same things Ellen was wondering:

- "Why should I even consider putting myself in an uncomfortable situation?"
- "My plate is already full, and I can't possibly take on any more tasks—so what's the payoff?"
- "What's the fuss? We're pretty busy. Why change?"

With all these concerns, you might be asking, like Ellen, why change? But consider this. What if you could turn eight out of ten difficult patients (or peers!) into people with whom you would always enjoy interacting?

Working with people you know and like would certainly make your job easier and more enjoyable. It makes for an all-around better day. If you were able to do that—with the help of some simple tools and without taking up any more of your time during the working day—would you be willing to give it a shot?

- What if we told you that you don't have to take it anymore?

- What if we told you that you can gain respect in what may seem at times a disrespectful environment? Are you interested in having more control over how your day—your week—your career—goes?

- What if we told you that you can be part of something bigger?

In Sandler Training, we often hear these concerns from support staff:

- "We're frustrated because we're spending less time solving problems and more time managing difficult people, and we end up doing neither very well."

- "We feel pressured to do more with less. Patients are more demanding, managers are asking more of us, our peers are becoming difficult, and we don't know how to express any of this to our superiors without sounding like we're whining."

- "We're tired of not gaining the respect we deserve and not being heard unless we yell and scream (which isn't our style)."

- "We're unsure of how to sell our ideas up the chain of command."

- "We're concerned that we're losing the drive and passion we once had in this job. We're burning out."

If you are a healthcare professional and you can relate to any of the above concerns, then you'll want to learn about what does work. You'll want to give it a fair shot. You'll want to decide for yourself whether it's worth trying.

For all of these players, going outside of the comfort zone and reinforcing new behaviors, attitudes, and techniques is where the magic happens. If you're intrigued by the possibility of making a difference, making a more fulfilling and rewarding contribution both personally and professionally, or being part of something bigger, then you'll want to learn more—not about what isn't working now, but about what does work once you accept the possibility of moving beyond the familiar.

CHAPTER 4

What Does Work

> When we are no longer able to change a situation,
> we are challenged to change ourselves.
> —Viktor E. Frankl

You'll recall my client George's complaint—that he'd already invested a whole weekend to train his staff in customer service and patient care. It's a fair concern. It's worth examining closely because at the heart of George's complaint is a reality that he and everyone else in the practice needs to understand: The training didn't work.

Why didn't it?

You can load yourself and your staff with scripts to recite, posters to study during coffee breaks, self-motivating mantras to repeat at your desks, will-power exercises, and a million little techniques to memorize and practice—and the training still won't work. Maybe some tiny bit of the training sticks, and perhaps an even tinier bit of it gets implemented in interactions with patients. But the critical outcome—the quality of the patient's experience—doesn't improve. Sometimes, it even gets worse. That's because all the scripts, posters, mantras, and techniques are useless if you don't step outside your comfort zone. People aren't inclined to step outside their comfort zone unless they have their inner game under control.

This is the part that is so often overlooked.

Let me introduce you to the inside-out game.

> *Training healthcare professionals to raise their game and perform at a higher level to deliver exceptional patient care is an inside-out game that requires peer support and ongoing reinforcement.*

I/R THEORY

No one likes to feel inadequate, nervous, embarrassed, or self-conscious. Most people like to feel that they have overcome these feelings. There's a sense of accomplishment and pride in achieving something difficult. The science behind this internal shift—from doing what's known and comfortable to doing the unknown and uncomfortable and feeling better about ourselves because of it—is called I/R Theory.

The "I" stands for your identity or self-worth, and the "R" stands for how well you perform the roles in your life. Your "I" and your "R" work together to define your comfort zone. But, it's the "I" in this pair that provides the horsepower to break free to try new things and to grow beyond the comfort zone for a more fulfilling and rewarding contribution, both personally and professionally. The "R" always follows the "I."

Let me take you through an exercise that we do with our clients, to put some meaning behind a person's "I" and his "R." You'll soon see why people's "I"—how they feel about themselves—drives their "R"—how they perform in their roles. It's this I/R pair that gently nudges people to move outside their comfort zone to a higher level—to where the magic is. This is the secret sauce behind Sandler's approach to training healthcare professionals to deliver exceptional patient care.

THE SAFE ZONE

Let's start by quantifying the power of your "I."

Start by visualizing a safe and comfortable place where there are no worries, no responsibilities, and no expectations of who you are and what you do. Think of a place where you are alone (by choice) and where you are most at peace. For some people, that may be a deserted tropical island with a warm breeze, soft sand, blue sky, and an ocean to float in aimlessly. For others, it may be sitting in your favorite chair in front of a crackling fire, with snow falling outside. No one can tell you what this special place looks like, feels like, and sounds like. That's your choice, and it's different for everyone.

Are you thinking of that safe place now?

Good. Picture yourself in this special place where you're at peace, you're alone, and you have no roles in life to play.

Maybe you're wondering, what do we mean by "no roles"?

We mean, in this safe place, you have absolutely no duties to fulfill as a parent, sibling, neighbor, manager, CEO, healthcare professional, or anything else. You are just you. You don't owe anyone anything. You have no job to do.

In this scenario, and in this state of mind, rate yourself on a scale from 1 to 10.

Now, before you pick a number, understand that an 8, 9, or 10 means:

- "I believe I can and will be successful at whatever I choose to do."
- "I always take responsibility for my actions and my results, even when it doesn't turn out positively."
- "I regularly set goals for myself and achieve them."

- "I like myself, my surroundings—my life."

Also understand that a 5, 6, or 7 means:

- "I see myself as average—not so bad, but not exceptional either."
- "If I set goals, they're modest, and I meet them."
- "My results and my actions are sometimes caused by me and sometimes due to the actions of others—it depends."
- "I have good days and bad days—and that determines whether I like my life and myself."

Finally, understand that a 4 or lower means:

- "I never win or exceed at anything—it's just not in the cards for me."
- "The actions I take and the results I get are always in response to what someone else has done or is doing. It's usually not my fault or it's out of my control."
- "Life is not easy—I struggle to make it through the day."

Please don't turn the page until you've given yourself a numerical score between 1 and 10.

WHAT SCORE DID YOU GIVE YOURSELF?

Having done this exercise thousands of times, we find that most people rate themselves in the middle (5, 6, or 7). When we ask them why, we hear some very honest feedback, such as:

- "I usually start out my day as an 8 or 9, but then I run into a difficult situation, patient, or co-worker. That brings me down a few notches."

We also hear the opposite, which sounds like this:

- "I'll start out my day as a 6 or 7, and then something externally happens during the day—I get recognized for a job well done by a boss, patient, or co-worker, or I get a compliment from a spouse or friend—and that raises me up to an 8, 9, or 10."

Very often, we hear a general statement like, "How I rate myself depends on how the day or week is going at the time."

Here's the moral of the story: Everyone is born a 10.

Was that hard for you to agree with? If so, read it again. Everyone is born a 10, and that's where everyone belongs. Yes, that means you, too.

All humans on the planet were born without any predefined roles, responsibilities, or expectations that determine their value. They were all born with the potential to do whatever they set their minds to do. Yet, as they grew up and their roles got defined (by family, society, geography, etc.), they started rating themselves based on how they performed in these roles. They sometimes let others' opinions of them determine their own sense of worth—their "I."

Let's put some meaning now to the "R," or your roles. Let's distinguish the "I" in your world from the "R" in your world.

On a separate sheet of paper, jot down all the roles you play in all aspects of your life. For example: parent, sibling, neighbor, volunteer, coach, etc.

How did you do? Your sheet is probably filled with roles like these:

- Sibling
- Parent
- Neighbor
- Caregiver
- Employee
- Leader
- Team Member
- Voter
- Bowling team member
- Runner

See how it works? Those are all roles you play. You might run your best mile on a certain day and give yourself a 9 as a runner, or you might run your worst mile and give yourself a 1. Either way, you remain a 10 as a person—as a growing, aware individual whose value isn't tied to how well you ran or how well you performed that day in your other roles.

Now, let's connect some dots between I/R Theory and the concept of the comfort zone to see why a change in outlook can fuel a breakthrough from mediocrity to excellence.

THE BREAKTHROUGH

The first principle that comes out of I/R Theory goes like this: People can only perform in a manner that they see themselves conceptually. Said another way: How you feel about yourself—your "I"—directly impacts how you will perform in your roles.

If you don't believe (for instance) that you can express appreciation to a patient without sounding fake or "salesy," then you won't begin the process of making yourself more comfortable in this role and you won't actually try it. You may fool yourself into thinking your "I" isn't high enough for you to do this. Actually, it's a role you can take on, not unlike an actor accepting a movie part. You can improve the performance over time, just as an actor does.

Similarly, if you can't envision yourself walking into a waiting room and standing next to a patient, with all eyes on you, to guide a patient back toward an exam room, then you won't perform this way consistently until you feel more confident doing it. Again, you may imagine that you yourself are operating at a 3 or a 4 (or lower) the first time you do this. Actually, it's just practice within the role. You're still a 10, even if you don't realize it in the moment.

If you don't feel comfortable saying to a new patient, "I'm glad you made it here today—welcome to our practice. How can I help you?," then you'll continue greeting patients in a way that's comfortable for you, which probably sounds something like this: "Hi, can I help you?" Quick question: If you were the patient, which greeting would you prefer to receive?

Here's the point. If you don't have the self-confidence—a high "I"—to try something new, let alone to be the first to try something, then you'll continue doing what you're doing now because it's more comfortable that way. You may even say to yourself, "At least I smiled," or, "At least I made eye contact," or, "At least I'm doing what everyone else is doing." That's a recipe for a mediocre patient experience. "At least" puts the interaction squarely within your comfort zone.

At Sandler, our approach to training healthcare professionals is unique and successful because we get to the heart of the matter. We strengthen people's inner game—their "I"—so that they're comfortable performing at a higher level—their "R." We help people step outside their comfort zone to manage new and difficult situations in the ever-changing healthcare field. That's the only way to get exceptional patient care to work—and to stick.

Let's get started.

TO GET MORE OF WHAT YOU WANT, GIVE THEM MORE OF WHAT THEY WANT

CHAPTER 5

Who Wants What?
An Overview

> Take care to get what you like or you will be forced
> to like what you get. —George Bernard Shaw

t's easy for healthcare professionals—for anybody, really—to fall into the trap of thinking: "If only I could change that other person." Or even: "I know I can't change that other person—in fact, there's no hope for anything changing for the better—so, I'm just going to do what I always do in this situation." If you're honest with yourself, you have to acknowledge how tempting it is to think that way when you're dealing with a difficult situation or person.

There are two unexpected truths to consider about these responses. First, when you respond like that, even without saying anything out loud, you are, yourself, increasing the difficulty of the situation. In a very real sense, you are creating difficult situations, people, and patients. Second, you have a lot more control over the situation than you think you do—if only you make the decision to harness the power of your own *why*.

Sometimes Sandler trainers will tell people on the first day of one of our courses: "If you came here thinking that you would get a silver bullet or a magic spell or some special phrase you could use to make somebody else change, you came to the wrong place."

Usually a silence falls over the room at that point.

Then we say: "On the other hand, if you came here because you want to learn how to manage difficult people and you're willing to accept that you are part of that process, if you're open to learning what you need to do differently to produce a better outcome, then you did come to the right place."

Where does that learning start? It starts with accepting that most of what we're about to share with you isn't hard, expensive, or earth-shattering. As you're about to see for yourself, it is entirely feasible for anyone to make the personal changes necessary to create and sustain an extraordinary patient experience in the healthcare field. Yes, it's rare—but it can be done, and it is a good deal easier than you may think.

So here's the million-dollar question: If truly delivering a *wow!* patient experience is feasible and good for business, why aren't more medical practices making it a priority? Why is it that the great ones are the only ones doing it? The answer is pretty simple: You have to overcome force of habit. Sometimes human beings let what's familiar and comfortable get in the way of what's possible.

Here's what's possible for your practice right now, today:

- If the healthcare team gives patients more of what they want, then the team will in return get more of what they want.
- What's more, if the healthcare team gives each other more of what they want, in the end everyone will get even more of what they want.

It's a great arrangement. Everyone who decides to play gets something back in return. But there's a catch.

You have to know what you want.

You have to dig deep and remember your personal *why*—your own reason that motivates you to move beyond what's familiar and into what's possible. You have to know what you want and why getting it is worth making a few easy (but not instantaneous) changes.

Go outside of your comfort zone long enough to learn what you need to do to give people what they want and you will get what you want from this job. Stay inside your comfort zone and stick with what's familiar—looking at other people and wishing they were different, calling them "difficult," sharing your favorite horror stories about them—and you will keep getting exactly what you're getting right now.

> *Unless you have a big enough personal why, unless you know what you want as a result of showing up each day for work, you won't be motivated to move out of your own comfort zone. Difficult people (patients and peers) will stay difficult. It's that simple.*

In the pages that follow, this book will address both what patients want (because that's what you have to focus on every day as a healthcare professional) and what your team wants (because that's what makes going outside the comfort zone worthwhile). You'll need to look at both sides of the equation if you want to transform the dynamic that underlies a difficult exchange with a patient. That's really what this is all about.

Let me give you some background here. Whenever Sandler trainers engage with a medical practice to train and coach healthcare professionals, we find the most popular training topic is how to manage difficult people. Hands down, that's the favorite "hot button" issue. That's what people want to hear about. That's the problem that occurs to people as needing to be solved.

After spending many hours myself in the field, I can

understand why this is such a big issue. It's not easy to deal with difficult people day after day. Let's face it: The medical field, by nature, attracts, welcomes, and must find a way to interact with a lot of potentially difficult people, starting with patients (who by definition are there usually because something is going wrong). Here's the challenge: The patient sees medical professionals as the ones being difficult. The interactions can become a tug-of-war, and guess what? Someone always loses.

> *A difficult you + a difficult them =*
> *a really difficult situation.*

We can tell you from our experience that healthcare professionals are passionate about solving patients' health problems. Not only that, they're good at problem solving. They were trained to solve problems, and they spend most of their day doing just that.

They're also deeply empathetic and compassionate people by nature. That means they genuinely like to help people, which is probably why they gravitated to the healthcare field in the first place.

Now, in a perfect world, most healthcare professionals would already have the skills and attitude in place to manage difficult people and situations whenever they arose. Unfortunately, this is not a perfect world. People face pressure to do more with less. Every day, it seems, there are more rules and regulations being mandated in the healthcare field, complicating the process of delivering care. As if all that weren't enough, patients have more choices than ever before. As a general rule, they can and do choose where and when they go for non-emergency care. As a result, they demand more for their money.

Medical practices must deal with all of these challenges and, at the same time, find a way to operate at peak performance to stay profitable.

In the end, healthcare professionals do their best to get patients in and out, avoid conflict if they can, and solve as many problems as possible. On a good day they leave feeling accomplished. On a bad day, they struggle to maintain control and end up feeling exhausted after eight, ten, twelve, or more hours of planting their feet, holding their ground, and pulling their end of the tug-of-war rope for cooperation.

That's the world they face. Now let me ask you a question: What about the patient? What do you think patients want?

THE PATIENT'S PERSPECTIVE

When I inquire about this during training sessions, participants often respond by asking this question: "Shouldn't the answers and solutions we provide be enough to make our patients cheering fans of our practice?"

If that's your thinking, please take a moment right now to think back over the past year or so. Think about all the medical appointments you've gone on as a patient. If you're like most people, you've had at least one visit that stood out amongst the rest as being an exceptional experience—and at least one visit that has you cringing and balling up your fists in anger, disappointment, or embarrassment.

The first experience and the second experience were very different, right? Even if your immediate medical issues were solved both times, you still developed two different impressions.

So I'm thinking you will probably agree with me when I say that the key to turning patients into cheering fans is not simply solving whatever medical problem they have. The whole experience is what counts.

Here are some of the things patients say that they want that we believe are controllable—see if you agree.

- **Patients want to feel appreciated and be acknowledged.** They don't want to be taken for granted. They know they have choices, and they expect extraordinary service. When they don't get it, they can become difficult. Often when patients walk into a doctor's office, they're treated professionally and respectfully but rarely appreciated.

- **Patients want to know what to expect each step of the way to calm their fears.** All too often, healthcare professionals assume the patient knows the routine as well as they do. They skip over explaining what will happen during the visit and why, who they will see, and how long it will take. Patients are left feeling anxious, worried, and maybe even frustrated. They may express these feelings outwardly to you or inwardly to themselves as they sit quietly in their seats. Either way, they're not cheering about the experience.

- **Patients want to feel OK.** They don't want to feel embarrassed, rushed, pressured, anxious, worried, or humiliated. Who does? Again, think back on your own experience as a patient for a moment. Your patients' experience is likely quite similar to yours. Before you, as a patient, even walk through the medical office door, you're probably feeling not-OK, either because you're in physical pain or discomfort, you have uncertainty about your health situation, or both. If you feel you're only being treated as a problem to be solved, you will feel more not-OK. This usually manifests itself in your showing impatience, complaining, asking an inordinate amount of questions, interrupting, refusing to follow directions, being uncooperative, not listening, feeling disappointed, and vowing to change doctors—in other words, being difficult. It's exactly the same for your practice's patients.

WHAT DO WE MEAN WHEN WE SAY "OK"?

According to transactional analysis, the school of psychology on which Sandler Training is based, there are four psychological positions from which a person can approach life. Which position you choose to hold has profound implications for your experience of life. The positions are:

- **I'm OK, and you're OK.** This is the healthiest position for everyone. It means that I feel good about myself and that I also feel good about others.
- **I'm OK, and you're not-OK.** In this position I feel good about myself but I see others as damaged or "less than."
- **I'm not-OK, and you are OK.** In this position I see myself as the weak partner in the relationship; I see you as definitely better than I am.
- **I'm not-OK, and you're not-OK.** This is the least healthy position of all. Everyone loses. I am in a terrible state, and the rest of the world is just as bad.

All discussions in which you transform a difficult patient into a patient you love dealing with come from the "I'm OK, and you're OK" position. This is an important principle of Sandler Training, and I will expand on the OK/not-OK principle in Chapter 9.

When patients are difficult, the day becomes a constant tug of war. Both sides struggle to maintain control, causing frustration, stress, and anger. This results in an unpleasant situation that can set the mood for the rest of the day. It can have a ripple effect in that you may pay it forward by unknowingly passing your not OK-ness to your peers in the form of being demanding, uncooperative, or sulky.

> *A difficult patient + a difficult healthcare professional =*
> *a really difficult work environment.*

THE HEALTHCARE PROFESSIONAL'S PERSPECTIVE

Of course, when you talk about what patients want, you are looking at things from the patient's side. What about from your side? You're probably thinking about something you want. Here are some examples of personal *why* objectives that we've heard from healthcare professionals.

The Staff Member's Perspective

What does staff member Ellen Everywhere want? She wants

less stress; she wants a productive way to deal with difficult people (patients and peers); she wants to be part of something bigger; and she wants a way to take better control of how her day, her job, and her future turns out.

The Doctor's Perspective

What about Dr. Raina Rapport? She wants to deliver a *wow!* patient experience—one that has patients cheering on social networks, in neighborhoods, on sports fields, everywhere—that drives a profitable, sustainable business. She wants to leave behind a legacy of great care standards when the time comes for her to retire.

The Leader's Perspective

Finally, what does George Upward want? Peak performance from his staff, A-players on the team, high morale, profitability, cheering fans, autonomy, and a seat in the boardroom. However, he's not likely to get any of that if his staff members aren't getting what they want, his doctors aren't getting what they want, and his patients aren't getting what they want.

The truth is, each healthcare professional may have his own personal, "What's in it for me?" (or WIIFM), but the common threads that run through the entire cast of characters in any workplace operating within the healthcare field are that everyone wants to feel appreciated, everyone wants to understand what's going on, and everyone wants to feel OK.

So what can you do to make sure they feel that way?

CHANGING THE PARADIGM

The remainder of this book will be about putting flesh on the bones of this principle of giving patients more of what they want in order for all healthcare professionals to get more of what they want.

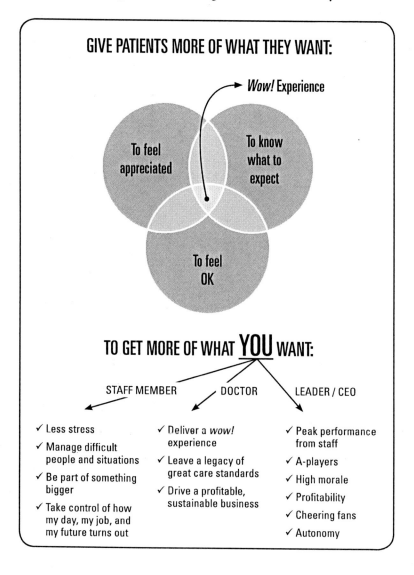

GIVE PATIENTS MORE OF WHAT THEY WANT:

Wow! Experience

To feel appreciated

To know what to expect

To feel OK

TO GET MORE OF WHAT **YOU** WANT:

STAFF MEMBER   DOCTOR   LEADER / CEO

✓ Less stress
✓ Manage difficult people and situations
✓ Be part of something bigger
✓ Take control of how my day, my job, and my future turns out

✓ Deliver a *wow!* experience
✓ Leave a legacy of great care standards
✓ Drive a profitable, sustainable business

✓ Peak performance from staff
✓ A-players
✓ High morale
✓ Profitability
✓ Cheering fans
✓ Autonomy

We here at Sandler Training have come to believe that this principle is the solution to the problem of how to run a great medical practice that has patients cheering and staff engaged. We have worked with hundreds of healthcare professionals, helping them to deliver a *wow!* patient experience every time.

In the next part of the book, we'll show you how to give in order to get—even if you've only got a very short time to do it.

CHAPTER 6

Only Treat Patients You Know and Like

> *There are no strangers here, only friends you haven't yet met. —William Butler Yeats*

ave you noticed? When a healthcare professional knows and likes the patient, building rapport with the patient comes easy. It's enjoyable and comfortable. It's hard for either side—patient or healthcare professional—to be difficult. However, when the healthcare professional doesn't know the patient, then building rapport can be uncomfortable—and it's easier for either side to be difficult.

In fact, when healthcare professionals already know and like a patient, they will automatically give that patient extraordinary care. It comes naturally to them. They don't even think about it, and everything falls into place.

Is there anything about this "know and like" relationship that can be bottled and used to build a bond faster when you don't know or like a patient? Is there a way to guarantee that you only treat patients you know and like?

THE NAME GAME

Let's begin with names. It won't come as a surprise to you to learn that, once you know and like people, you probably know and use their names, typically their first names, more often than if you don't know them. A person's name defines that individual. A name is one's identity. It's personal.

It's only logical then that if healthcare professionals master the name game by introducing themselves by first name and using the patient's first name, they'd be on their way toward building a bond with the patient. Common sense and probably life experience tell you that if you know and like someone, you're less likely to be difficult—you're more likely to be on your best behavior. Learning someone's name is a critical early component of getting to know that person.

Think about the last time you were driving your car and running late. You probably had to make some choices about who you would squeeze past in order to get to your destination faster.

(I'm sure all of those choices were legal!) Here's my question: If you were driving on the highway and running late, would you squeeze in front of a neighbor you know and like? Would you pass that person on the one-lane back road that leads to your home, accelerating around without so much as a nod or a glance?

Probably not. You know and like that neighbor, and you wouldn't drive "like that" in front of him.

To repeat: When you know and like someone on a casual level you're generally on your best behavior. Not only that, it generally is easier and more natural to be on your best behavior. (This is distinct from knowing someone intimately—a family member, partner, or best friend—which can sometimes bring out people's worst behavior because they've "let their hair down." Luckily, most people don't cross this line as working professionals.)

Imagine this scenario. Pretend your name is Donna.

You're the patient visiting your doctor's office. Ellen Everywhere, the staff member in charge of bringing you back to an exam room, walks up to you, makes eye contact, smiles, and says, "Donna?" politely, while she's standing near you in the waiting room. You nod and stand. She offers you a sunny, "Good morning, Donna," and then says, "I'm Ellen. I see you are here to see Dr. Rapport. Welcome to our practice. Let's get you started in an exam room."

How do you feel? Pretty good, right? Let's continue.

Ellen walks with you into the exam room, gestures toward
a chair, and asks you if you want to take a seat. She smiles
that sunny smile again, then says, "Donna, Jamie at the
front desk may have mentioned to you that Dr. Rapport is
running about ten minutes behind. Dr. Rapport is aware
of it, and she's quickly getting caught up. In the meantime,
let me take your blood pressure and your temperature.
We do this first with all our patients." After she completes
those procedures, she says, "Do you have a favorite magazine that I can get you to read for the next few minutes?"

Now how do you feel? Still pretty good, yes? Of course, you're
not exactly ecstatic that the doctor is running late—who would
be?—but compare the experience I just shared with you to the
following experience, which is much more common.

The healthcare professional (Ellen) stands in the doorway
leading to the exam rooms and calls out your name. You
stand and walk to where she is. She says "Hi, I'm Ellen.
How are you? Follow me, please." You follow her to the
exam room. She gestures toward a chair and says, "Let me
take your vitals." After she's done so, she says, "The doctor
will be with you shortly," and leaves.

When healthcare professionals use names—theirs, the
patient's, the doctor's—it makes the experience more personal.
 eople involved are no longer strangers. As we've established,

it's a little harder to be difficult with someone you know in these kinds of situations. There's more at stake.

It's often easy to be difficult to a stranger—there's little risk of consequence in saying or doing something disrespectful or unkind. You have no personal connection to that person, and you may never see him again. The small act of exchanging first names moves the relationship quickly from stranger to acquaintance—from difficult to cooperative. Try it and see.

Bottom line: Introducing yourself (first name is usually enough) is the single best way to bond with someone in one second or less.

CHAPTER 7

The One Thing You Need to Know to Manage Difficult People

> *The opposite of anger is not calmness; it's empathy.*
> —Mehmet Oz

W hen I was right out of college, I landed a job at an aerospace company. I worked in the computer/IT department doing everything from programming to managing email servers—and, in retrospect, managing difficult people. Once a week I had to take my turn at the help desk and answer any and all computer-related questions that came in from company employees.

The engineers and scientists who worked there were solving

mission-critical problems so if their computers or the software running on them didn't work, they couldn't work—and if they couldn't work, they reached out to the help desk in what can only be described as a state of panic.

I learned a big lesson about customer service, and I learned it the hard way. The lesson was this: If I let myself act difficult in a difficult situation, then I created a difficult hour—day—maybe even a week—for myself.

Which, it turned out, I was pretty good at doing. In fact, for the first few months, I dreaded my days at the help desk. The dread dragged me down. When someone called for help, my habit was to mimic their reaction and start playing by their rules, not mine.

So: If they called in a panic, I would go into panic mode, too. In my case, that meant I would stop listening and start solving. If they called in a rush, I reacted by interrupting and stepping on their words—so I could fix the problem more quickly, I told myself. If they criticized and complained, I became defensive.

There was a common thread to all of these conversations: As the person calling me got more difficult, I got more difficult— and my days (and life!) got more difficult.

My help-desk peers and I would commiserate about how disrespectfully we were being treated—they needed us, and look at how they treated us. We thought we had only two choices: stay and take it, or leave. This left me in a quandary. I wasn't prepared to leave—and I was tired of taking it.

One day, a mentor pulled me aside and gave me the one tool I needed to better manage these difficult people and situations. I agreed to do as he suggested, which was to try the validation principle for five seconds each time.

How hard could that be?

THE VALIDATION PRINCIPLE

On paper, the advice he passed along sounded quite simple. I remember thinking, "Well, that's going to be easy." In real life, it was harder than I imagined because doing it required me to (you guessed it) go outside my comfort zone and change my habits— my knee-jerk reactions.

But I had promised to try it his way each time for five whole seconds. I think I agreed to do that because I was frustrated that my life felt outside my control. I was tired of other people determining whether I'd have a good or bad day. I was concerned that my destiny wasn't my destiny at all, and I was frustrated that others seemed to be charting it. Not only that—I was letting them.

Here's what he wanted me to do. I should pause before jumping in with an answer and simply acknowledge or validate—out loud—how the other person was feeling. In total, this took about five seconds.

For instance, by saying, "I can understand why you'r

frustrated by this. I would be too under the circumstances. I can help." I didn't have to make it up—it was quite clear how the other person was feeling (frustrated, panicked, concerned, worried, or rushed) and I knew I could help.

It took a little practice—remember, I had weeks and weeks of habit that pointed me toward cutting the other person off, jumping in, and solving the problem right away. But eventually I learned to begin the conversation as my mentor had suggested. The difference it made was absolutely astonishing.

Validating the other person's emotional state changed the tone—for the better—of the exchange. You might think that saying something like, "I can understand why you're frustrated by this," was conceding defeat. You might think that empathizing with the other person, when you're the one getting beaten up, would put you in a position of weakness. Actually, though, those five seconds, once I learned to use them properly, were the exact opposite of defeat. They certainly didn't signal weakness. On the contrary—they created a position of strength from which I could act.

It's easy to react with an emotion—angry, impatient, annoyed, defiant, victimized, sulky—when you're in the presence of a difficult person. It takes a lot of strength and discipline to remain calm and composed and not react emotionally—instead, to pause and acknowledge how the other person is feeling. But this is the single best thing anyone can do to manage difficult people.

The validation principle is simply recognizing and then acknowledging the other person's emotional state, whether or not you agree with it. This principle works really well with patients. Let's take a look at why that is so.

Normally, when a patient has to deal with a long delay while waiting in a pretty good (but not great) medical practice, what happens? The timid patient gets no information whatsoever, and just waits—stewing—until he is summoned to the exam room. Not a great experience. The braver patient ventures over to whoever is manning the front desk and asks what's going on. At that point, the patient hears, "We're sorry, the doctor had some emergency. She'll be with you shortly." Not a bad experience but not a great experience, either.

What would happen if front desk employees empathized with patients—timid or brave—and told them that they understand it can be frustrating to wait?

Before you dismiss that possibility, let's imagine what would happen.

You walk into the waiting room, and it looks really crowded. You ask at the front desk how long it's going to be. The person there says something like:

"I can see that it's going to be about 20 or 30 minutes before Dr. Rapport sees you. I know that's probably the last thing you want to hear, Mike [your first name]. V have three doctors on for today. The waiting room lo(

a little more crowded than usual, but we've got the staff on site to handle it. Dr. Rapport knows she's behind and is working to get caught up. Rest assured that when she sees you, she's going to give you her full attention. In the meantime, let me suggest a few things you can do while you're waiting—"

Wow!

That kind of response doesn't always come as second nature. You and your staff may have to practice it a bit. But that time you spend practicing will be time well spent. What would happen if one of the healthcare professionals at the practice circulated through the waiting room every few minutes to check in on people and give them status updates? We're not saying you need to do a standup comedy routine. But we are suggesting that you find a way to give people something to focus on that isn't, "Sit there and wait and don't make a fuss (because we're more important than you are)."

Let's face it. If you put people in a difficult situation that they can't control and then you ignore their emotional state, you can expect people to be difficult. In fact, that's how people become difficult. If your goal were to create as many difficult patients as you could, what would you do? You would keep information from them, take away their control, make them wait, and ignore their emotional state. That would turn Mother Teresa into a difficult patient.

You can't change the fact that the doctor had an emergency. You can't change the fact that a medical test is taking a little longer than you thought. You can't change the fact that patients were booked back to back, intentionally or by mistake. You can't change the fact that there was a last-minute addition to the schedule. Those are things you can't always control in a thriving medical practice.

But what you can control is the quality of the experience that patients have while they are waiting to see the doctor. It's your job to figure out how to make that wait a pleasant experience for patients—and ultimately for yourself and your staff. To make that happen, you have to go outside your comfort zone. Not only that, you have to make sure you are surrounded by peers who will support you as you go there.

Change the paradigm.

Disrupt the pattern.

Make it a pleasant experience and not "a wait."

Try it. You'll see what we mean. You will learn that if you give patients what they want, which is often simply to be validated, you will get what you want—more cooperation, less confrontation, more respect, less push back, more dignity. It's a win-win.

But there's a catch. To pull this off, you need to put a pretty high value on yourself. You have to feel like you can say and do what we're suggesting. You have to see yourself doing it. You have to step outside your comfort zone and raise your "I" to an 8, 9, or 10.

Consider the following scenarios, which anyone working in a medical practice is likely to hear frequently.

DIFFICULT PATIENT (frustrated): "Is it going to be much longer? I've already been waiting 15 minutes!"

Now consider these two possible responses.

HEALTHCARE PROFESSIONAL with a low self-value (7 or lower): "We're doing our best. We'll be right with you."

What's really being said: "Sit down like everyone else and wait your turn."

HEALTHCARE PROFESSIONAL with a high self-value (8 or higher) (pauses for half a second, nods): "I understand your frustration. I'd be frustrated, too. The doctor got off to a slow start because of an unplanned emergency. She's aware of the inconvenience to her patients, and she's quickly getting caught up. At this point, there are two patients ahead of you. I can keep you posted, if you'd like."

What's really being said: "You matter. What you're feeling is valid. We're here for you."

Here's another example:

DIFFICULT PATIENT (embarrassed): "I'm confused about some of the questions on the forms I have to fill out. Like [pointing to a field on a form] what does this mean?"

HEALTHCARE PROFESSIONAL with a low self-value (7 or lower): "Just do your best to answer the questions."

What's really being said: "You're not doing your best—sit down and try again."

HEALTHCARE PROFESSIONAL with a high self-value (8 or higher): "Some of these questions can be confusing. Let's take a look together."

What's really being said: "You matter. What you're feeling is valid. You can do this."

By the way, exactly the same dynamic comes into play during exchanges with difficult colleagues or peers in the practice. Let's take a look.

DIFFICULT PEER: "That's not my job responsibility!"

HEALTHCARE PROFESSIONAL with a low self-value (7 or lower): "I know, but we're all doing our best around here, and we expect everyone to pitch in."

What's really being said: "You are not doing your best and you are not pitching in—and we are. Therefore, you are failing."

HEALTHCARE PROFESSIONAL with a high self-value (8 or higher): "You're right, and I feel funny asking you to take on more responsibility when your plate is pretty full. For whatever reason, there's more work and less time today. If things change at your end, we could use the extra hands in helping us get through this."

What's really being said: "You matter. What you're feeling is valid. You're needed."

DIFFICULT PEER: "Arlene, get over here. I need you right now!"

HEALTHCARE PROFESSIONAL with a low self-value (7 or lower): "OK, I'm here."

What's really being said: "My opinion doesn't matter—you can just order me around."

HEALTHCARE PROFESSIONAL with a high self-value (8 or higher): "We were huddled over there discussing a scheduling conflict, but that can wait. You sound like you have something more urgent for me."

What's really being said: "I matter. What I'm feeling is valid, but so is what you are feeling. We'll solve this together."

Notice that, in these higher exchanges, both participants get what they want. The patients or difficult peers get validation, and the healthcare professionals feel good because they managed a difficult situation effectively.

You know what? This works with everyone, not just difficult people.

CHAPTER 8

How to Gain Respect (in a Disrespectful World)

> *When you show deep empathy toward others, their defensive energy goes down, and positive energy replaces it. That's when you can get more creative in solving problems.*
> —Stephen Covey

et's acknowledge a basic reality of today's world. When a patient and a healthcare professional come together, it's quite common for the patient to feel not-OK about something.

That's true for you when you're a patient; it's true for me when

I'm a patient; it's true for the people who walk into your practice. There is a seemingly endless list of likely reasons for patients
to feel not-OK as they sit in the waiting room: the long wait, the
anxiety about their personal health, the frustration of trying and
failing to decipher what is and isn't covered under their healthcare plan, the concern of missing work or time away from their
family, the physical pain they're in, the nuisance of dealing with
their insurance company, the disruption of their day for them to
show up for the appointment in the first place—and on and on.
You could probably add another dozen or so items to that list
from your own personal experience.

A not-OK feeling can sometimes rear its ugly head and lead a
patient to act disrespectfully toward the messenger of whatever
update he's getting. Have you ever done that as a patient? I know
I have.

In the scenario below, Ellen, the professional at the front
desk, is doing her best to get patients in and out. She's not out to
cause problems. She's avoiding confrontation, and frankly, she
wouldn't mind just plain getting through the day. But she doesn't
yet have the tools—or the comfort level—necessary to manage
difficult people. Let's listen in on the following exchange.

ELLEN: Hi. How can I help you?

JUSTIN (impatiently): I'm here to see Dr. Rapport.

ELLEN: OK, what's your name?

JUSTIN: Justin Smith.

ELLEN: OK, Justin, please fill out this paperwork—both sides—and have a seat. We'll be right with you.

JUSTIN (irritated): Why do I have to fill out all this information again? Nothing has changed since my last visit.

ELLEN: All of our patients have to fill it out. We want to be sure to have all of your current information.

JUSTIN: Why do I have to fill out the insurance information? Here's my insurance card. Why can't you do it?

ELLEN: We'll need you to fill it out, sir—it's important we have your current insurance information on file.

JUSTIN (sighs): How long is the wait?

ELLEN: The doctor is running just a few minutes behind today—it won't be long.

JUSTIN (dismissively): Look. I'm in a hurry. Can I reschedule?

ELLEN: There's really no need to reschedule. If you can have a seat and fill out this paperwork—both sides—I can help the next person.

JUSTIN (stomping away): This is ridiculous!

Sound familiar?

It doesn't end here. More and more patients are talking about their healthcare experiences using social media. So, a bad (or even mediocre) experience can take on a life of its own—and live on for a long, long time.

Imagine having several difficult interactions similar to the above in just one week—or even one day. Most people can't do the job of a healthcare professional. Today's healthcare professional must stay sharp on the technical aspects of a job involving life-and-death decisions and be able to manage the difficult feelings, concerns, and questions that go along with these emotional decisions. It's a demanding job, and not many people are up for it. Only a small percentage are willing and able to do what they do.

Was Justin disrespectful? Of course. Does that make him the enemy? No. Let's make a few simple changes to the above scenario to help Ellen manage a disrespectful situation. As you'll see, the opening seconds of the interaction make all the difference. This brings us to a vitally important point: How the conversation starts will set the tone for the rest of the conversation.

ELLEN: Hi, my name is Ellen. Welcome to our practice. How can I help you this morning?

JUSTIN (impatient): I'm Justin Smith and I'm here to see Dr. Rapport.

ELLEN: Hi, Justin. Let's get you started right away and have you fill out some questions—it takes just a few minutes. There are questions on both sides of these sheets. I know the last thing you probably feel like doing is filling out paperwork—we don't like it either. We have to stay current with your information so we'll need you to help us.

JUSTIN (irritated): Why do I have to fill out all this information again? Nothing has changed.

ELLEN: That's a good question; I'd be wondering the same thing, Justin. We're just not sure if anything has changed about you since the last time you were here, and this form helps us figure that out.

JUSTIN: Do I have to fill out the insurance information if you have my insurance card?

ELLEN: I know the insurance information can be tedious to enter. How about this? If you can enter these two fields, we'll fill in the rest from your card.

JUSTIN: OK. How long is the wait?

ELLEN: Our waiting room looks pretty crowded this morning, but we have four doctors in the office today helping our patients. We'll get you in and out as fast as we can. There are three patients ahead of you. Dr. Rapport is aware that her patients are waiting, and she's quickly getting caught up.

JUSTIN: Ugh—I'm in a hurry. Can I reschedule?

ELLEN: I can help you to reschedule if you prefer. I'm wondering what's easier for you—to keep this appointment since you're already here, or to start all over again with a new appointment. What would you like to do?

JUSTIN (thinks it over): I'll wait.

How many differences did you spot between the first scenario and the second?

Did you notice how Ellen took control of the interaction at

the start? In doing so she set the tone for the rest of the conversation. She started off by introducing herself and welcoming the patient to the practice, in spite of a crowded waiting room full of patients. The tone she set was for a respectful, peer-to-peer conversation with the patient. Each and every step of the way she made a point of making Justin feel good about himself, especially when he showed frustration. She kept the tone from becoming a tug of war with each side vying for control.

We've implemented the second scenario many times with our healthcare clients, and there's no debate that it makes for a better patient experience than the first scenario and a less confrontational experience for the healthcare professional. However, we're not suggesting that the healthcare professional's approach in the second scenario will always result in a cooperative patient. Our experience is that it works about 80% of the time. The other 20% of the population of patients will be difficult no matter what.

Offering an exceptional patient experience and being able to manage eight out of ten difficult patients is enough for most healthcare practices to change their patient-care approach from good to great. They find that the return on their investment is a strong one.

It gets better, though. We discovered two additional positive outcomes when the healthcare professional took on the challenge of turning a difficult patient into a cooperative one. First, the majority of healthcare professionals ended their day with a higher "I," meaning a higher self-esteem because they felt in control of their day and felt a sense of accomplishment being able to manage a difficult situation. It didn't matter whether or not the patient remained difficult or whether or not "it worked"— either way, the healthcare professionals had a better day because they had a healthier way of handling difficult people that didn't involve reacting emotionally nor taking it.

This translated into a second bonus—higher morale in the office and less overall stress. The bottom line: It became the "new normal" to consistently treat patients with extraordinary care because it came back around to the healthcare professionals in the form of a higher level of performance and a better sense of personal satisfaction in the job.

CHAPTER 9

Patients Want to Feel Good about Themselves

> *If you would lift me up you must be on higher ground.*
> *—Ralph Waldo Emerson*

T ake a moment to think back on your own experiences with bonding and building rapport with another person. If you make people—patients or otherwise—feel good about themselves, isn't it naturally easier to bond with them?

There's actually science behind this principle of human interaction. It can be found in the book, *I'm OK—You're OK*, written by Dr. Thomas Harris. Through extensive research and studies, Dr. Harris concluded that most people are not-OK about themselves or their surroundings. He also concluded that most people want to feel OK.

You may remember this OK/not-OK concept from Chapter 5. Let's briefly review what OK and not-OK feelings are—and then do a deeper dive so we can put real-life meaning behind them.

What do people mean when they say they are feeling OK? Feeling OK is being able to say to yourself, "I feel pretty good about myself and my surroundings. Life isn't perfect, but I'm hopeful things will turn out for the best. I almost always take responsibility for how things turn out."

How about the opposite end of the spectrum? Feeling not-OK can be a persistent feeling that never seems to go away, or it can come and go with some frequency (daily, weekly, situationally, you name it). A not-OK feeling is one or more of the following: embarrassment, resentment, anger, anxiety, nervousness, confusion, frustration, uncertainty, or feeling pressured, worried, stressed, uncomfortable, incompetent, or dismissed, etc.

It's not that OK people never have not-OK feelings—they do. The difference is they take responsibility for doing something about their not-OK feelings in a way that doesn't make someone else not-OK in the process. They say to themselves, "I've got this!," and they mean it. They choose to leave a not-OK state as soon as possible.

YOUR OWN OK AND NOT-OK MOMENTS

Let's look at the way this breaks down specifically. Take a minute and reflect back on yesterday, the past week, and last month. If you're like most people, you have felt one or more not-OK feelings at some point recently. For some, it's not that frequent. Some people spend more time feeling OK than not-OK. For others, the scale tips more on the not-OK side.

- Get some clarity right now about a specific time when you were definitely feeling OK.
- Now, get equally clear about a specific time when you were definitely feeling not-OK.

Big difference, right? These were probably two very different worlds for you. They certainly are for me.

Guess what? It's the same for patients. It's the same for everyone. There are big, noticeable differences between feeling OK and feeling not-OK. The trick is to begin to notice when you're in each state. Then you can do a better job of helping others.

WHY ALL THIS MATTERS

Maybe, as you were looking at those two situations, it occurred to you what some of those differences between feeling OK and feeling not-OK really were.

Here's what the healthcare professionals I work with usually find. When interacting with a not-OK person—patient or colleague—they find that the not-OK person tends to be less cooperative, more defensive, less open to hear suggestions, more difficult, and probably less likeable. The chances of building trust and bonding with a person who is feeling not-OK are pretty low unless you can take control of the situation and make the not-OK person feel better—more OK.

You would think it takes a lot of time and energy to make another person feel better about himself. But, we find that most of the time it takes very little work to make someone feel more OK. Most people—98%, according to Dr. Harris—want to feel OK. Yes, that number definitely includes patients. After all, who wants to feel embarrassed, worried, stressed, frustrated, or concerned? Most people are searching for small but significant ways to feel better about themselves, their situation, or their surroundings.

So, the question is not, "Am I OK or not?"; it's, "When I feel not-OK, how long will I stay in that state?"

When you address not OK-ness this way, you can start to redefine your job when it comes to interacting with patients. In the past, you may have thought that your first and most important job was to get information from a patient, make sure a patient's records are up to date, get a patient logged into the system, or help a patient get the care he needs. Don't get me wrong. Those are all extremely important things to do. However, how about trying on the possibility that it's just as important (in non-emergency situations) to help your patients move closer to feeling OK?

If you can open yourself up to that possibility, you're going to find that it's easier than you thought—and that it gives you a big advantage, in the marketplace and everywhere else. It makes the day easier for everyone. It gives you far fewer difficult patients to deal with over the course of the week. If you keep it up, it creates an experience that leaves patients cheering.

ANOTHER PIECE OF OK/NOT-OK

There's another important dimension of this. Sometimes people try to make themselves feel more OK by making someone else not-OK.

This is a quick fix—a temporary fix—and it can even feel like it's justified. Let me give you a personal example of what I mean. Sometimes, after a long day at work, I would come home and spend time with my husband, talk through what happened during the day, and, if the day had been particularly stressful, start to gossip about our friends, family, or neighbors. It seemed like a good way of dealing with the challenges I was facing because I usually felt a little better afterwards. My challenges didn't seem so bad after gossiping about my neighbors' challenges. For a while, I thought that kind of talk actually brought me closer to feeling OK. But it didn't. It was like having a sugar fix. There was a short-term boost, and then a longer-term drop. Of course, to compensate for that drop, there was a temptation to find more people to make not-OK behind their backs.

Here's the problem. I wasn't owning up to the problems I was facing. Instead, I was deflecting them onto innocent bystanders. One of the elements of feeling OK is taking responsibility for your outcomes in life—good or bad. When I talked about people behind their backs, this was the opposite of my taking full responsibility for my outcomes—for how my day went and how I was feeling. If I had a problem with someone or something, the best way to have dealt with it would have been to take the problem to the person who could best help me solve it. If a situation made me upset, the best way to have dealt with that would have been to ask myself what I could do differently to improve the circumstances.

I mention this because one of the important criteria for feeling OK is accountability. If you're blaming someone else for your situation, you're probably feeling not-OK (though you might be forgiven for imagining you are just fine). In the case of gossip, no matter how good it might make you feel in the short term, you're scoring points at someone else's expense and making someone else responsible for how you feel.

It's probably unrealistic to expect anyone to completely abandon chatting about others—most people do a little gossiping here and there. But I mention gossip in the context of noticing whether you're accepting full responsibility for your outcomes because it became an unhealthy coping mechanism for me. The problem is, it just manufactures feeling better about yourself—a faux OK feeling—when you find yourself in a not-OK moment. Changing that one behavior dramatically increased the amount of time I spent feeling OK—not just a little, but a lot. I want to be sure you know that, if you find yourself in a similar situation.

This issue of gossip applies in any workplace. In fact, it's sometimes one of the reasons we at Sandler get called to talk to teams in the first place—not to lecture on the wrongs of gossip, but to help the healthcare professionals understand why it's occurring, how they're coping with it, and what to do about it.

CHAPTER 10

Small but Significant Ways to Make Someone Feel OK

> *I can live for two months on a good compliment.*
> *—Mark Twain*

Here are our favorite small-but-significant approaches to making others feel more OK. Master these approaches and you will become great at making others, notably patients, feel better about themselves—and ultimately get more of what you want.

ACTIVE LISTENING

Consider the following scenario to help illustrate the difference between listening and hearing.

You come home from work one night to Robin, the beloved spouse or significant other who is always there to greet you. "Robin," you say, "you wouldn't believe what a day I had. The phone was constantly ringing, the lines in the waiting room were ten deep most of the day, and, if that wasn't enough, two people called in sick. I didn't even get to eat lunch. I'm beat!"

All the while, Robin has been attentive—looking right at you and making eye contact. When you finish, Robin responds with, "That sounds pretty stressful. Let me tell you about my day..."

How would you rate Robin's listening skills? Robin did in fact hear what you said by setting aside everything else that was happening and being attentive. There was that nice acknowledgement that your day was stressful. But was Robin really listening? How do you know Robin didn't tune out after five seconds?

Let's try this again.

You come home from work one night to Robin, the beloved spouse or significant other who is always there to greet you. "Robin," you say, "you wouldn't believe what a day I had. The phone was constantly ringing, the lines in the waiting room were ten deep most of the day, and, if that wasn't enough, two people called in sick. I didn't even get to eat lunch. I'm beat!"

All the while, Robin has been attentive—looking right at you and making eye contact. When you finish, Robin responds with: "It sounds like you had a hectic day. You couldn't catch a break, could you? I bet you just want to relax for the rest of the night."

In the first scenario, Robin was hearing. In the second, Robin was listening. You can tell because the empathy you got was specific to what you said and to how you were feeling.

Hearing and listening are the same in that they both use our ears. They're different in that while hearing is more of a science—even computers can recognize and decipher our speech—listening is more of an art. Computers aren't all that good at reading between the lines. Thank goodness you get to interact with people as people—not as computers. Thank goodness you can listen. But it takes conscious effort to do so.

One particularly effective way to let the other person know that you are listening is by relaying back or paraphrasing what you heard. Think of paraphrasing as extracting the key points that you heard and restating them in your own words. You won't want to mix up paraphrasing with mimicking. A parrot mimics—repeating back, word for word, what it heard. A computer can do that, too. But that's not listening.

Let's take an example from a medical practice.

ELLEN: So what brings you in to see us today?

PATIENT: Well, the other day, I was out pulling weeds in the garden, and I think I pulled a muscle. I felt a twinge, and the pain just hasn't gone away. Now it's affecting what I can and can't do with the kids. They're running me ragged, and I can't keep up.

ELLEN: OK. The doctor will be with you in a minute and decide what he wants to do.

There's nothing really wrong with that exchange. But how could we make it even better? Take a look at this as one possibility.

ELLEN: So what brings you in to see us today?

PATIENT: Well, the other day, I was out pulling weeds in the garden, and I think I pulled a muscle. I felt a twinge, and the pain just hasn't gone away. Now it's affecting what I can and can't do with the kids. They're running me ragged, and I can't keep up.

ELLEN: I understand—it's so easy to pull a muscle. You must be exhausted. I have three kids of my own. I can only imagine what that must be like when you're not feeling well. Good thing you came in. I'll bring this to the doctor's attention.

You can show that you're paying attention by demonstrating the very best body language—sitting undistracted, looking the other person in the eye, nodding every once in a while—but that's not the same thing as showing that you're listening. In your head you could be thinking about your day, what you're going to have for dinner, or what you'll say next. Most people simply want to be heard. They want proof that you've been listening while they share what's important to them. Sure, they're looking for answers and solutions, but they can get that from a lot of sources, including the internet. From you, they want proof that someone understands them.

STROKE, STRUGGLE, VALIDATE

There are three tools that are particularly effective and easy to use in making people feel good about themselves: stroke, struggle, and validate. (You've already gotten an introduction to validation in Chapter 7.) You can use one, two, or all three of these tools in interactions with patients—it depends on the situation.

A stroke is a small, genuine compliment (notice that it's not gushing praise) in response to something the other person said or did. It's intended to make the other person feel good about himself. It's all too easy to get off on the wrong foot with a patient when you omit giving a stroke. Take a look:

PATIENT: I did some research online, and I think I know what's wrong with me.

HEALTHCARE PROFESSIONAL: We don't recommend you self-diagnose. You can't always believe everything you read online. The doctor will have a better idea of what's going on after examining you.

What's really being said: "You were wrong to do that—shame on you." Here's a better exchange:

PATIENT: I did some research online, and I think I know what's wrong with me.

HEALTHCARE PROFESSIONAL (responding with a stroke): I'm glad you brought this up. It's helpful to know what you think is going on. Let's hear what you found out.

What's really being said: "Your opinion matters. You didn't do anything wrong. I'd like to hear what you think."

Here are some other stroke examples.

In response to a question from a patient that the healthcare professional has heard a million times:

HEALTHCARE PROFESSIONAL (responding with a stroke): That's a good question—one we hear quite often.

What's really being said: "You're on top of things. You ask important questions."

In response to the question from a patient, "What should I do next?"

HEALTHCARE PROFESSIONAL: Let me run a few ideas by you that have worked in similar situations, and then we can talk about what would work best for you.

What's really being said: "You know yourself best. I respect your opinion. Let's find something that works for you."

A struggle, on the other hand, is being a little not-OK (but not to the point that you're appearing incompetent or unconfident). When people are not-OK—which most people are—they feel better when they're sharing their not OK-ness with someone who also isn't super OK. Think about it for a minute. If you're not-OK and you're sharing the situation with someone who has it all figured out, you might wonder why it's not so easy for you. You might wonder why you can't be more like that super-OK person. You might wonder what's wrong with you. In the end, you feel even more not-OK.

Here's an example of communication with a patient that does not use a struggle—and ends up making the patient feel less OK than when he started:

PATIENT: I know I should be staying off my leg so it can heal. I'm just so frustrated that I can't exercise anymore. It's really getting to me. So I'm running a little bit here and there.

HEALTHCARE PROFESSIONAL: If you want to heal, you'll want to do as the doctor recommended, which is to stay off it for a month.

What's really being said: "I don't care how frustrated you are. We know best. Do as you're told."

Here's a better response using a struggle.

HEALTHCARE PROFESSIONAL: Knowing how much you get out of exercising, I can see why you're frustrated. Let me make sure I understand everything so we can find a solution that works for you. Is it OK if I ask a few questions?

What's really being said: "You didn't do anything wrong. I may not understand fully so let's try this again."

Here's another example of an exchange without the struggle, the stroke, or the validation:

PATIENT: I would like to see the doctor as soon as possible. Monday morning, first thing, is the best time for me.

HEALTHCARE PROFESSIONAL: The doctor isn't available on Monday. In fact, he's booking appointments three weeks from now.

What's really being said: "I don't care what works best for you. This is the best we can do."

Here's a better response:

HEALTHCARE PROFESSIONAL: It sounds like you have an urgent concern [note the validation statement] so let's see how soon we can get you in. I'm looking through the appointment calendar now. I see that the doctor is booked pretty solid [here's a struggle], but if you can stay with me on the phone a few minutes, I'm trying to find a way we can squeeze you in as soon as possible. Let me run a few options by you. [Here comes another struggle.] They're not perfect but they may work for you.

What's really being said: "I hear you. Your request is not unreasonable. I'm struggling here to find the perfect solution. I have a couple ideas that could work."

Here are a few more good examples.

In response to a complaint by a patient for something that the healthcare professional listening had no part in:

HEALTHCARE PROFESSIONAL: From what you're telling me, I'd be frustrated, too. Thanks for sharing this story with me. I'll get to the bottom of it.

What's really being said: "Based on your side of the story, you have good reason to be frustrated. We want to know about these situations so we can fix them. I'm on it."

In response to a confusing question asked by a patient:

HEALTHCARE PROFESSIONAL (responding with a struggle): I'm not sure I understand. Would you mind explaining for me?

What's really being said: "It's my misunderstanding. Let's try this again."

Give others what they want—to feel OK (better about themselves and their situation)—and everyone will end up feeling more OK. Don't take our word for it—try it and see for yourself.

CHAPTER 11

Patients Want to Know What to Expect

> The single biggest problem in communication
> is the illusion that it has taken place.
> —George Bernard Shaw

t my client Upward Medicine, Ellen Everywhere was skeptical at first when I suggested that there was a simple technique that could help her manage the stress that comes with working in a busy, thriving medical practice—a technique that she could learn to deliver in just a few seconds and implement easily the next time she walked into work.

She wasn't convinced that the simple change in behavior I'd

shown her could have as much benefit as I had promised, but she agreed to give it an honest try for two weeks. What did I show her how to do? Set expectations with her patients and her peers.

When we saw each other two weeks later, Ellen shared with me that the simple practice of setting expectations with patients and even her peers had transformed her interactions. What had often been a confrontational dynamic instantly became a collaborative one. She had more control over how her day went. Her confidence grew because she was getting more of what she wanted—peace of mind, less confrontation, and less stress. In theory, it was simple to do; in reality, it meant going outside her comfort zone. The alternative—doing nothing and living with the stress—was more painful than the discomfort of changing her behavior. She soon became a master at the Up-Front Contract, the critical Sandler tool for setting expectations between two or more people in an exchange.

The up-front contract is particularly powerful in the setting of a medical practice. Why? Most human beings don't like surprises when it comes to visiting a doctor's office. They're already anxious about their health condition. All kinds of questions are coursing through their minds. "Why am I feeling this way?" "How can you help me?" "When will I start feeling better?" "What's wrong with me?" Adding more surprises that are unrelated to a patient's health condition can be the tipping point that turns a peaceful office environment into a stressful one.

If you're like Ellen, you may be skeptical that a less than

20-second change in the way you begin conversations can transform that dynamic. Before you file what we're sharing with you here under, "Sounds interesting, but it probably won't work in my world," consider the following.

We asked patients the question healthcare professionals are sometimes afraid to ask: "What makes you feel not-OK about your experience here?" You're about to find out some of the things that make them feel not-OK and maybe even make them act difficult. Get ready for some surprises. You will see things here that you may not have realized are likely to trigger seemingly irrational, unjustified negative exchanges. It is only when patients feel that they have no control over their world that they get difficult. Here is what makes them feel like they have no control.

- Showing up for an appointment on time and waiting patiently for 20 minutes, only to be told that the doctor is running late because of an unforeseen problem. Then the wait is another 10 minutes.
  ◊ Patients are frustrated, wondering why no one had the courtesy to tell them when they first got there.

- Waiting patiently for 10 minutes and watching patients come in after them and being called before them; then, going up to the front desk to ask if someone forgot about them only to find out that more than one doctor is on duty that day and they're up next.

◊ Patients feel stupid that they spent 10 minutes worried that someone forgot about them. They're embarrassed in front of everyone (other patients included) that they overreacted. It was unnecessary and could have been prevented if someone had just told them the status.

- Leaving a voicemail message with the doctor's office (for example, sharing some information that they forgot to share at their visit that morning) and being concerned that without this information, the doctor is going to misdiagnose their condition and drag things out. Hours go by. They call back a second and third time because they're only getting voicemail—only to find out later that every voicemail message is listened to within 30 minutes of coming in and the office staff members address the concern even if they don't call back right away. Furthermore, all calls are returned by the end of the day.

  ◊ Patients are embarrassed or maybe even angry that they left three urgent messages, not knowing that someone heard the first one within 30 minutes of leaving it. The doctor's office was "on it," and planned to call back before the end of the day—but no one told them that.

- Being escorted to the exam room, anxious to see the doctor or the assistant and to talk about their concerns only to find out that they have to get a procedure (e.g., an X-ray, blood work) first, before they get to see the doctor. They're wondering: "Will insurance cover this? Why is the doctor asking for an X-ray or blood work? Is something wrong that the doctor isn't telling me?"

◊ Patients feel stupid when they find out afterwards that this is standard procedure—that having a pre-exam procedure actually gives the doctor the information he needs to better assess what's going on. If only someone had told them!

The common thread in all of these situations comes down to this: If patients would have been told what to expect, they would have been more understanding and less difficult, less likely to leave the practice, and less likely to write a negative comment on social media.

Any reasonable person understands that doctors can get caught up in a medical situation that takes longer than expected. A crowded waiting room doesn't mean the doctor is running late, voicemail messages can't always be returned instantaneously, and medical professionals know what's best. But understanding and rational thinking tends to evaporate when people are kept in the dark about what's going on. They may even say to themselves, "Why didn't they just tell me up front what's going on? What else are they keeping from me?"

If you're a healthcare professional then your practice

undoubtedly experiences the unexpected on a daily basis. You'll find the up-front contract very useful.

The up-front contract is a short script that's used before the unexpected happens, with the single purpose of setting expectations to diffuse a potentially uncomfortable situation down the road.

The up-front contract has five parts. At first glance they may appear canned or even fake. But once you understand the spirit of the up-front contract, you'll be on your way toward customizing it so that it feels genuine, flows easily, and fits your personality. The five parts of a strong up-front contract are:

1. Show appreciation.
2. Deal with time.
3. Acknowledge what the other person is expecting.
4. Explain what you expect.
5. Get confirmation that you're both on the same page.

Here's a version of an up-front contract that could be used by a medical professional who ushers a patient from the waiting room to the exam room.

HEALTHCARE PROFESSIONAL: Keiko?

KEIKO: Yes, that's me.

HEALTHCARE PROFESSIONAL (using a mini up-front contract): Good morning, Keiko. My name is Ellen. I work with Dr. Rapport, and I'll get you started with your visit today.

KEIKO: OK, thank you. Let me collect my stuff.

They walk from the waiting room to the exam room.

HEALTHCARE PROFESSIONAL (using a longer up-front contract): Welcome to our practice, Keiko. I'll be spending the first few minutes with you, to collect some information for Dr. Rapport, including your blood pressure and temperature. Keiko, I know you may have some questions that are on your mind today. You can ask me. If I can't answer them, I'll be sure to have them ready for the doctor when she sees you. Dr. Rapport is finishing up with a patient now, and will be ready to see you next. Shall we get started?

KEIKO: Sure.

Once vitals are done and before leaving, the healthcare professional says something like:

HEALTHCARE PROFESSIONAL: I have everything I need at this point. Is there anything else you want to share with me before I leave?

If you timed the above up-front contract—and I have—you would find it takes less than 30 seconds. That's a tiny time investment for delivering a *wow!* experience. All it takes is a little practice.

Let's remind ourselves what a typical scenario looks like without an up-front contract when a healthcare professional ushers a patient from the waiting room to an exam room.

> *The up-front contract is not meant to interfere with the operations of a busy medical practice. It's not meant to add to anyone's workload, and it's certainly not meant to make matters worse. The purpose of the up-front contract is to set expectations and diffuse a potentially difficult situation down the road.*

HEALTHCARE PROFESSIONAL: Keiko?

KEIKO: Yes, that's me.

HEALTHCARE PROFESSIONAL: Hi. How are you?

KEIKO: Good, thank you.

HEALTHCARE PROFESSIONAL: Let's head back to the exam room.

KEIKO: OK, thank you. Let me collect my stuff.

They walk from the waiting room to the exam room.

HEALTHCARE PROFESSIONAL: What brings you here today?

KEIKO: I've been having pain in my side, off and on for a week now.

HEALTHCARE PROFESSIONAL: OK, the doctor will take a look when she sees you. Let's take your vitals.

Once vitals are done and before leaving, the healthcare professional says something like:

HEALTHCARE PROFESSIONAL: The doctor will be right in.

Assuming you received the same excellent medical care at both practices, which experience would have you writing glowing reviews on social media? If you're an owner or leader of a medical practice, which experience makes you proud? Which scenario would you like to experience as a patient?

CHAPTER 12

It's Not What You Say but How You Say It

> *I've learned that people will forget what you said, people will forget what you did, but people will never forget how you made them feel.*
> *—Maya Angelou*

After reading about the up-front contract, you might be a little curious about how it would actually work in your practice. You might even be thinking about memorizing what I just shared with you as a script, or asking someone else to memorize it.

Unfortunately, that's probably not going to accomplish much.

The problem is, you can't do an up-front contract that's worthy of the name without first establishing a peer-to-peer relationship. This kind of relationship is very different from when one person is the authority figure and the other is expected to follow orders.

The sad reality is that healthcare workers are used to playing the role of the authority figure. If you memorize a script for an up-front contract but deliver the words of that script as though correcting an errant child, you'll end up doing more harm than good.

Why does this happen? It's not because those in healthcare are bad people. It could be how they've trained themselves over the years to get through the day. Could it be that simple? Just as important—could they have been wrong? Is it possible that taking on the role of authority figure makes the day more stressful, not less?

Let's take a step back and see how and why professionals could have trained themselves to communicate this way.

WHAT IS PEER-TO-PEER?

When you have a productive, healthy relationship with someone over the long term, that is a peer-to-peer relationship.

In this kind of relationship, you're both listening, not judging. You're focusing on what you can do together, as opposed to what the other person should do. You seek first to understand where the other person is coming from, before you make your point.

You're focused on possibility—you're curious—and therefore you don't make assumptions.

Our friend Ellen Everywhere wasn't used to doing that. So when she was told that creating a peer-to-peer relationship, as defined above, was a necessary preliminary step to setting an effective up-front contract, she needed a little time to get her head around that. She was used to dealing with patients in a very different way.

To put it bluntly, she was used to being completely in charge of the relationship. She was used to sending body language signals to patients (and colleagues) that said, "Don't look at me, don't interrupt me, I have things to do. I'm more important than you are." She would talk to people while on the phone or dealing with paperwork, and she responded to perceived threats by doubling down on the ego state that transactional analysis calls the Critical Parent. This is the voice from your past that scolds, that corrects, that disapproves—and it's all too easy to use. That voice is very different from the voice of the Nurturing Parent, who supports, encourages, and engages, or the voice of the Adult, who focuses on facts, logic, and rationale.

Much of what Ellen did and said during the day was coming from the Critical Parent and addressed the patient or peer as though that person was in the role of the Child. The problem with Critical Parent-to-Child exchanges is that they're unproductive and unhealthy.

Take a moment to glance back at your childhood and think

about a situation when you were being criticized by an adult. Now reflect on how it turned out. Did you both walk away feeling better having talked about it? Or did you retreat to your room and pout? Did you respond defensively? Did you respond with a temper tantrum? Did you cry?

Yeah. Me too. Let's consider the possibility that Critical Parent is not the optimal voice to use with a patient—or a peer—or anybody, for that matter.

The first point I make to people like Ellen—the point they generally agree to try on as though trying on a new garment—is that while starting exchanges from the Critical Parent position is easy, it also creates more drama than they need and it can be exhausting by the end of the day.

Let's face it—keeping up the tug-of-war, participating in an endless series of debates, always trying to prove you're right, defending yourself, your actions, and your medical practice, over and over again, can wear you out. If nothing else, it's exhausting because it's difficult to keep track of where you left off.

Here's the second point I make to Ellen-types: An effective up-front contract will never happen if you attempt to establish it from the Critical Parent.

A third point: Sometimes you get so used to sending subtle signals—both spoken and unspoken—that identify you as the Critical Parent that you need some practice and some time to turn that around.

When one Ellen-type I worked with tried that idea on, she made a commitment to work on changing the pattern. Thirty days later, she was the practice's reigning expert on establishing peer-to-peer relationships. The up-front contract was one of her go-to communication tools.

If you're willing to try on the same three ideas—1) that the Critical Parent role is exhausting and more trouble than it's worth, 2) that visual signals and tone of voice can send disapproving Critical Parent messages that make it hard to bond with patients and peers, and 3) that the reasons for sending those messages aren't as compelling as the reasons to invest some time and energy to create a new pattern of behavior—then you will soon find yourself getting somewhere wonderful in the first minute or so of your exchanges with patients and colleagues.

Equally ineffective (and unhealthy) is the Child voice. This is the voice from your past that responds too emotionally to a situation. The Child shows up as too angry, apologetic, sneaky, manipulative, excited, silly, sulky, pouty, etc. It includes all the emotional reactions you would expect from a child but not from an adult in a mature situation.

Imagine yourself talking to an older person whom you respect—for example, a parent or grandparent. How would you raise a sensitive topic with that person? What kind of tonality would you use? What words would you choose? How would you confirm that you had landed your point?

Now imagine yourself raising an equally sensitive topic with a young person you know well—a teenager or a young adult. If you're like most of us, you're a little less likely to raise the topic in question carefully, to monitor the young person's reaction to what you have to say, and to use a positive stroke of some kind during the exchange.

Why does this matter so much? Well, in the first instance, it was likely that you had established a productive peer-to-peer exchange where both parties walked away from the discussion feeling good about themselves and headed in the right direction. In the second instance, maybe not so much. People are likelier to go into inappropriate communication mode when they're dealing with a younger person. Unfortunately, they can slip into this habit with lots of other people, too—without even realizing it.

Establishing a peer-to-peer relationship and communicating as equals, especially when there's an age difference or a role difference, is a critical skill set that can make a big difference. We find that teaching a topic like peer-to-peer is best done face-to-face and can rarely be learned by reading a book. It takes time, persistence, support—and a lot of practice—to make and sustain changes in behavior. Learning how to create a peer-to-peer relationship in a matter of seconds is worth it.

CHAPTER 13

Patients Want an Experience to Rave About

> Time you enjoy wasting is not wasted time.
> —Marthe Troly-Curtin

O ne of the top reasons—if not the #1 reason—patients do not rave about their visits to the doctor has to do with time.

Here are some things we've heard from patients about the issue of time. As you read through them, consider how often you, too, have felt this way as a patient:

- "I had to wait much longer than I expected."
- "I spent very little time with the healthcare professionals and more time waiting."

- "I felt like a nuisance."

- "I didn't get all my questions answered."

- "I was kept in the dark about something important to me."

- "I felt rushed."

- "My phone call wasn't returned for hours—I was worried."

On and on. Sound familiar?

Some of these time issues can be fixed, but very often they can't. The unexpected happens often when you're diagnosing and treating the human body. Additionally, if your office is focused on running a profitable medical practice that hums with activity during the day, there will probably be very few time adjustments that can be made.

However, we have found that dealing with the "time thing" is better than ignoring it. Why? Here's where the medical field can steal best practices from successful businesses in the non-medical field. Take Apple Inc. retail stores, for instance. There are always lines there. Have you noticed? The stores are always buzzing with activity and crowds. It's rare you see customers get angry because of how they were treated. It's rare you see anyone turn around in disgust and leave, despite the appearance of a long wait.

What's Apple's secret? Apple retail stores interrupt the pattern of what the waiting experience feels like. In fact, Apple is so good at it, no one thinks to call the Apple store a "waiting room" at all. How can you apply that secret to your medical office?

INTERRUPT THE PATTERN

An extraordinary patient experience takes the patient out of the realm of the real world to a place where he's distracted from thinking about his condition, his state of affairs, how long he's already had to wait, or the reason for his visit. Your typical medical office waiting room, on the other hand, with bland music and a mundane TV show playing, conjures up bad memories of crowded airports, the school principal's office, and the line at the Department of Motor Vehicles.

Here are some approaches you can use to transform the waiting experience from good to great.

- **"We're glad you're here!"** Have you ever noticed what happens when you walk into an Apple retail store? Almost instantly, a team member or greeter notices you first, before you have to figure out where to go and who to see to check in. Before you can turn around and walk out, that Apple team member notices you and welcomes you.

- **"We're on it!"** Just showing appreciation isn't enough. Customers (and patients) want to know that they're in the system and they're moving forward in the line. The Apple greeter not only welcomes you, but also collects the information needed to get things rolling. Apple takes it a step further and displays your first name and your place in line on a digital screen so you know at any point in time exactly where you stand.

- **"We're looking out for you!"** Showing appreciation, getting you in the system, and keeping you in the loop on where you stand during your visit can all fall apart if you ever feel that you're being treated unfairly so you have to police the situation. Have you ever been to a doctor's office, patiently waiting your turn, when you notice that patients coming in after you are being taken care of before you? Think about the last time you were seated at a restaurant and you noticed tables seated after you getting their meal before you. Long wait lines or rooms that are not policed by someone in authority can bring out the worst in people.

Everyone wants to be treated fairly. But most people feel uncomfortable expressing frustration when they feel they're being treated unfairly. You may think that a silent and obedient patient sitting in a waiting room is unfazed by a long wait. You may think that silence is satisfaction, or at least consent. But you know what? More often than you might think, that silence belongs to someone who is uncomfortable expressing his frustration, anger, or even panic. The silent ones can and do turn into difficult patients. In fact, when you leave them on their own, it's as if you're saying to them, "Be difficult! We dare you!"

Here's the big lesson healthcare providers can take from Apple retail stores. Patients are rarely treated as customers—and they're pleasantly surprised when they are.

We're not suggesting that you have to do exactly what the Apple store does and redesign your space. What we are suggesting is that the time you do have is precious. Whatever time you've got available, you can use it in support of the patient, in a way that makes sense for your practice, to send the same basic messages:

- "We're glad you're here!"
- "We're on it!"
- "We're looking out for you!"

Here's one way to pull that off.

90 Seconds

✓ Actively listen to the patient
✓ Break the pattern of the "waiting" room experience

60 Seconds

✓ Set an Up-Front Contract
✓ Deal with waiting times

10 Seconds

✓ Convey appreciation when greeting the patient, and introduce yourself by first name

Hi, my name is Donna. Welcome to our practice.

✓ Use stroke/struggle/validation phrases to keep the patient OK

If you've got 10 seconds, greet patients by welcoming them to the practice in a genuine way that conveys that you know they have choices and you're glad they chose your practice. Share your first name, and then ask for the patient's name. Give a stroke of some kind (a small, genuine compliment or other positive communication). If patients show up not-OK, validate how they must be feeling, make it clear you too are struggling, and propose a next step. (Note: This is an art, not a science. It involves reading the person's tonality and body language and responding appropriately. Yes, you can do all this in 10 seconds or less.)

If you've got 60 seconds, do everything in the 10-second paragraph, and then also set an up-front contract that establishes what they can expect from their visit, including managing their expectations around time.

If you've got 90 seconds, do everything above and use active listening to show you are present—that you really are listening to everything the person says. Then break the pattern the patient typically experiences in a medical office waiting room. One suggestion is to bring a front-desk person out into the waiting room to greet patients as they enter, acknowledge those who are waiting with the status of their wait time, suggest things to do while waiting such as offering a beverage, a tablet for the internet, or a set of headphones to listen to music, or whatever feels best suited to your practice.

Whether you've got 10 seconds, 60 seconds, or 90 seconds

at your disposal—and that will likely vary based on the level of activity you're dealing with—the critical question is always: "How can I best invest that time to deliver an extraordinary patient experience?"

CHAPTER 14

The Five-Second Challenge

> Do the thing we fear, and death of fear is certain.
> —Ralph Waldo Emerson

W hether you're a healthcare professional or someone who manages a healthcare team, you may be saying to yourself right about now that this stuff won't work at your practice. You may even be a little curious how we pull this off at other practices. You may be thinking that these are all great suggestions but they will be uncomfortable for many of the people at your practice to do and will therefore be unsuccessful.

Well, you're in good company. These are pretty common and

understandable thoughts. What you probably want to ask is: "How do I perform (or get my team to perform) an uncomfortable task or behavior?"

My answer is this: Take it five seconds at a time.

If you knew you only had to be brave for five seconds straight, do you think you could? Would you be willing to do a task or behavior for five seconds, knowing that you'll feel better about yourself afterwards? Nine times out of ten when we ask this question, the answer we hear back is, "Yes!"

Following are a few examples of the kind of patient-experience behaviors that can be uncomfortable for many healthcare professionals.

GETTING COMFORTABLE WITH DISCOMFORT

For some people, introducing themselves to patients by first name can be quite uncomfortable. Although exchanging first names quickly moves a relationship from stranger to acquaintance—from potentially difficult to civil—if people at the front desk are stressed about managing a long waiting line, introducing themselves may feel like it will only take more time. Also, it feels awkward being so cheery and friendly to a patient who is frustrated by the long wait and anxious about the outcome of the impending doctor's visit. So, the front desk people might continue doing what they've always done, which sounds something like, "Hi, can I help you?"

However, when we work with professionals who are uncomfortable introducing themselves—usually because it's not a habit in their daily routine—we can get nine out of ten people to try it for five seconds.

Let's look at the process of ushering a patient from a waiting room to an exam room. If you're responsible for ushering patients, you may feel uncomfortable breaking the routine of how you've always done it, which is to call the patient to come to you as you wait at the door and then to lead him to the exam room. We find that a better patient experience is to walk up to a patient in the waiting room, introduce yourself by first name, and, if appropriate, shake hands. Then walk with him to the exam room.

"But," Ellen Everywhere might say, "ushering a patient the way I've always done it is now a habit. It's uncomfortable, and sometimes hard, to break a habit."

True enough. But what about a five-second test drive? It's rare that someone won't be willing to try it for just five seconds—especially in a supportive, safe environment with peers cheering him on.

Others have said things like: "If one of my responsibilities as a healthcare professional is to talk with potential new patients to answer their questions, then expressing appreciation for the opportunity to help and treat them makes me sound like a salesperson. I'm a healthcare professional, not a salesperson."

Yet, when we ask these same people if they'd be willing to try it the Sandler way for just five seconds, with a huddle afterwards to talk about what worked and what didn't, we almost always get a "yeah, OK" response.

It's human nature to resist doing something uncomfortable. People tend to resist because they think it will be long-term discomfort. But if you knew up front that the emotional pain would be five seconds tops and that the people around you would be supportive, you'd be more likely to do it. Once you realize that the five seconds wasn't so bad, you'd agree to another five seconds tomorrow—and then ten seconds the following day. Pretty soon you've raised your comfort level without experiencing a lot of pain all at once.

Ellen Everywhere was no exception. She flew through the five-second practice with flying colors—and was on the path to breaking through her comfort zone.

ACCELERATING CHANGE

As part of Sandler's patient-care training approach, we will very often accelerate change by going into the field to work side-by-side with healthcare professionals so they can practice what they've been learning in class. This gives us an opportunity to connect with people at a deeper level, walk in their shoes, and feel their discomfort for ourselves.

Very often, we will volunteer to be the first to try something.

We'll tell the team outright that we're feeling uncomfortable (because we really are!) with what we're about to do. We haven't done it before, and we're pretty sure it won't go exactly as planned. This, we admit, makes us feel inadequate—and we may even sound a little nervous. We'll ask them to time us doing it so everyone gains a better understanding of how long our discomfort lasted. We tell them that we'll debrief afterwards, discussing what worked and what didn't.

In all the times we've done this in the field, we rarely have a problem getting a volunteer to try the new way of doing things after we've gone first. Once people see us going outside our comfort zone for five seconds, they're more willing to give it a try. This may apply to your staff as well. If you go first, they will follow.

You may be wondering, "What about the doctors? Do they ever struggle with communicating more effectively with patients?" And the answer is, "Yes." Doctors are indeed eager to connect faster with patients to get to the root of the problem. But human nature can sometimes get in the way of an honest conversation between doctor and patient.

Imagine yourself as a patient during a doctor's visit, being asked a question you're uncomfortable answering truthfully, for whatever reason. If you're like most people in this situation, you won't look the doctor in the eye and give the doctor a 100% truthful answer the very first time out. You may tell a white lie or give a partial answer, or even change the subject. Why does that happen? It's not because patients want to drag the diagnosis out or mislead the doctor. More often than not, it's because they're embarrassed or worried or confused. They're not-OK, and this gets in the way of telling the truth about what's going on.

Doctors we work with want to be able to connect and communicate more effectively with patients to uncover the truth and therefore be able to do their job better. Of course, they want to communicate better with everyone else, too. All of the principles outlined in this book can be shared with people from all walks of life, including doctors. The difference is that the model for training doctors typically involves one-on-one sessions—as opposed to group training. We find this model to be more productive for doctors as we can customize the tools to fit their approach. The scheduling becomes easier for one-on-one training, too.

CHAPTER 15

Do-It-Yourself First Aid Kit for the Healthcare Professional

> *No one can make you feel inferior without your consent. —Eleanor Roosevelt*

We've seen how important having a high "I" (or sense of self-worth) is to successful, peer-to-peer interactions with patients and colleagues. I wrote this chapter because healthcare professionals often have to perform their own first aid when it comes to maintaining a strong personal sense of self-worth—a high "I"—during a busy day. Here are four do-it-yourself (DIY) tactics for protecting your self-esteem, confidence, and general wellbeing.

123

DIY TIP #1: EASE THE STING

When someone is rude, it can sting. Talking down to people, embarrassing them in front of others, speaking in a hostile or overbearing tone—these are just a few of the ways that rudeness can leave a mark. Much of the sting goes away, though, if you remember that a person's rudeness isn't targeted at you personally.

People who appear rude are usually emotionally charged about something—typically something that has nothing to do with you. It may feel personal to you because you happen to be in their line of fire. The minute you change your outlook and stop giving power to the rude person, you will find it doesn't sting as much. But when you react emotionally to a rude person or when you stand there and take it, you lose control and ultimately hand over the power.

Let's take a look at an emotionally charged situation between two healthcare professionals (Chris and Ellen) who are on a short break. Who's in control?

CHRIS: Do you think this Sandler stuff is really going to work? I honestly don't believe it's a good match for our environment, and I think I've been around long enough to know. A lot of other things have to change first.

ELLEN: Wow. I don't see why you're always so closed-mind to new things. Why don't you lighten up?

CHRIS: Get real. Nobody's taking it seriously—why are you bothering?

ELLEN: Please don't tell me what to do, Chris.

Not only is Chris in control, but Ellen is reacting defensively—which is one of the best ways to undermine a healthy, peer-to-peer dialogue.

Let's take the same situation and change how Ellen responds.

CHRIS: Do you think this Sandler stuff is really going to work? I honestly don't believe it's a good match for our environment, and I think I've been around long enough to know. A lot of other things have to change first.

ELLEN: Chris, you have been here longer than any of us, and you've definitely seen us go through a lot of changes.

CHRIS: That's the truth!

ELLEN: I know you've seen a lot of stuff come and go. Can I ask you something?

CHRIS: OK.

ELLEN: Well—I did try a few of these new communication tools we're learning. For whatever reason, I didn't feel totally comfortable with it. Would you be willing to listen to what I did and give me some feedback, based on your experience?

CHRIS: I guess. Sure, go ahead. Tell me what happened.

Now who's in control?

In the second example, Ellen took the lead and changed the dynamic of the conversation—without making Chris feel not-OK. Ellen didn't allow Chris to hook her into reacting defensively. She used a few well-timed genuine compliments, and she asked for feedback to lead Chris in a positive direction. Chris moved from complaining to collaborating.

DIY TIP #2: DEFEND YOUR CASTLE

Picture a towering stone castle with a wide, deep moat around it. In the days of castles and moats, there was only one sure way of getting inside the castle, and that was to come in by way of a lowered drawbridge. That was the cutting-edge technology of the day. You know what? It worked. Only someone inside the castle could lower the drawbridge. In setting it up this way, the rulers maintained total control over who could enter their castle—their kingdom. This secured their future.

Military technology may have changed a bit since the 1400s, but the basic idea behind the castle and the moat is still quite powerful.

When it comes to who you let in your head—your "castle"— you have the same inside control over the drawbridge that a reigning monarch would. Someone who is difficult or knows how to push your buttons can only get in your head if you lower the drawbridge and let him in. Once he's in your head, he's there until he either decides to leave (which he rarely does—after all, it's rent-free space) or you kick him out (which is easier said than done— the guest who overstays a visit can be tough to get rid of).

Who or what is in your castle right now that shouldn't be? Is it a peer or co-worker who talks about you behind your back? Someone who isn't doing a fair share of the workload? A superior who talks down to you or gave you negative feedback that's accurate—but still stings? An employee working for you who disrupts the whole team? In these examples, defending your castle means not stewing over these people or situations in your head. It also means not complaining to others about it (which can easily slip into gossiping). It means not letting the situation hit your "I"—your identity, or how you feel about yourself.

Keeping your drawbridge up and locked can mean moving on and letting the person or situation go. It can mean giving the other person a little room to be himself. It can mean being open to the idea that you contributed to the situation in some way and owning up to that. It can also mean looking inside your castle and reflecting on what you could do to make the other person OK, regardless of who is right or wrong.

You will always know if someone or something is in your castle. The tipoff is simple: You're feeling not-OK. Likewise, you'll know if your drawbridge is up and locked when you're feeling OK about yourself, about the person, and about the situation.

The moral of the story is this: People who don't belong in your castle shouldn't be able to talk you into lowering your drawbridge.

DIY TIP #3: KNOW YOUR WIIFM ("WHAT'S IN IT FOR ME")

You've probably heard it said before, "If you want something to get done, give it to a busy person." Why is that true? A person who is not busy has enough time to think, "I can always get that done later." A busy person, on the other hand, says, "I better get this done now, or it's not happening!" The non-busy person is usually working for someone else's goals or responding to someone else's emergency. By contrast, a person who is busy has typically planned out the day to the minute. That doesn't mean the busy person is selfish. Far from it. The busy person's plan usually includes specific ideas about the very best ways to give others what they want. What's different is that the busy person has a game plan that corresponds to an important personal goal. If you ask this person, "What's in it for you today at work?," you're going to get a clear answer.

Do you have personal goals for yourself in your role as a healthcare professional? Have you considered how you might be able to reach those goals if you helped others (patients, coworkers, managers, shareholders, doctors) reach theirs?

Here are some goals that healthcare professionals have shared with me:

- To gain the respect and loyalty of the doctors in the practice.
- To be acknowledged as an A-player.
- To be promoted to a leadership role.

- To keep a job they enjoy doing so they can support their family.

- To be included in decision making for the practice.

It shouldn't come as a surprise that the owners and stakeholders of a medical practice have the goal of running a profitable business by delivering a *wow!* experience to a maximum number of patients each week. How does your answer to the question, "What's in it for me?" support and align with that kind of big organizational goal?

Here are a few examples to consider:

- Volunteer to mentor an employee who is struggling, for whatever reason, with the goal of delivering a *wow!* experience.

- Implement daily or weekly "huddles" with the team to reinforce patient-care best practices.

- Write a short blurb for your company newsletter or internal website about a *wow!* experience you witnessed at your practice.

- Be a role model for how to deliver an exceptional patient experience.

DIY TIP #4: BLOW OFF SOME STEAM

This is primarily a tip for teams who work in a fast-paced, thriving healthcare practice. The hours can be long and the stress le can sometimes be high. One suggestion for ensuring that the team as a whole (and each individual member of it) maintains a strong, positive sense of self is to schedule group events outside the workplace where people can enjoy each other's company and build relationships. This is one of those little steps that, if taken once a month or once a quarter, can have a huge impact on the team's morale.

CHAPTER 16

The Team

> *For the great doesn't happen through impulse*
> *alone, and is a succession of little things*
> *that are brought together.*
> *—Vincent Van Gogh*

've shared a lot with you in this book, and some of it might seem counterintuitive. In fact, I'd be willing to bet that, right about now, you've come across enough in these pages that feels unfamiliar and uncomfortable, and maybe even unworkable, to make you strongly consider putting these ideas away for a while—just to "think about it."

Please don't. Take the initiative. Take action. Start learning about and internalizing these principles in person. Start the journey that moves you from, "This feels uncomfortable," to, "This is what I do." Do that for the sake of your team. Every touch point adds to or detracts from the patient experience. Patients have to give a little, too, of course, but at the end of the day, you come together in support of each other as members of a team.

Imagine if 80% of your practice's healthcare professionals made one change based on what you read in this book. Imagine what it would mean for the patients, the practice, and the healthcare professionals. Imagine what it would mean for how your day and week and life goes.

The sad truth is that most medical practices operate in a way that makes working days more difficult than they have to be for the people who spend their days there. It's not out of any desire to do so, but rather a failure to execute ways to make it less likely that you will encounter a difficult person.

You have to approach this as a team.

It's much harder for everyone when patients slip into difficult mode. You may fool yourself into believing that you have no control over that. But the truth is that you do have control over it—far more control than you imagine. That control starts with how you interact with each other.

If you're interested in transforming your practice, a great

resource is Sandler Training. At the end of this book, you'll find a low-pressure, easy way to test drive Sandler. Check it out.

At the end of the training process, we promise you will have a toolbox for delivering a *wow!* patient experience. You will understand how to give people what they want to get what you want. What you do with that toolbox and this new knowledge about human behavior is up to you, of course. But if you use the tools in the way they were designed, you may be surprised at what's possible.

EPILOGUE

Is Doing Nothing an Option?

> *Insanity: doing the same thing over and over again and expecting different results.*
> *—Anonymous (widely, and inaccurately, attributed to Albert Einstein)*

I still remember the moment Dr. George Upward decided to work with Sandler.

Toward the end of our first face-to-face discussion, I asked him a question that caused him to take a deep breath, purse his lips, and bring his closed fist to his lips. That question was: "George, what happens if you do nothing?"

He stared off into the distance for a long time.

"What if," I continued, filling the silence, "nothing changes to raise the quality of both the patient experience and the comfort level of the healthcare professionals who work for you? What if patients continue feeling frustrated and anxious about their experience at your medical practice and the healthcare professionals continue to be in a perpetual state of overwhelm with the stress of dealing with difficult people? What if your medical practice looks like this today—and tomorrow—and the next day—and next month—year after year?"

When the conversation finally got going again, George and I had a nice talk about, of all people, the actor Bill Murray.

GROUNDHOG DAY

In the 1993 movie *Groundhog Day*, Bill Murray plays a TV weatherman—Phil Connors—who has a general dislike for people. He is uncomfortable about his assignment covering the annual groundhog festivities in Punxsutawney, Pennsylvania. Phil is uncomfortable about interacting with the small-town people in Punxsutawney. He is uncomfortable working with his peers on this assignment. Likewise, no one who interacts with him on this fateful Groundhog Day is comfortable having to work with the arrogant, unfriendly, disrespectful Phil Connors.

As Phil and his team are getting ready to leave Punxsutawney, a snowstorm hits and shuts down the town, forcing everyone to stay another night. Phil wakes up the next day and finds that he is reliving Groundhog Day all over again. The day plays out exactly as it did before, with only Phil's choices of how to respond subject to change. Only Phil is aware of this. He faces the same familiar events the next day—and the next—and the next. Every day is Groundhog Day! Phil grows more and more depressed the longer this goes on, until he is inspired to change his attitude and his daily behaviors to break outside his comfort zone.

This choice allows him to have a positive influence on the people he interacts with during the day. His inspiration is a woman—Andie MacDowell, playing his producer—who emerges as the film's love interest. All Phil's attempts at winning her over fail, day after familiar day, until he finally comes to the realization that he has to challenge his comfort zone in order to get what he wants. Just doing it the way he's done it before can't get him what he wants—he has to change his behaviors and give the woman he loves what she wants to get what he wants. Thus the time loop is broken.

As we talked about this movie, George got the connection right away. A lot of medical practices—his included—find themselves in something very similar to Phil's predicament.

Sandler has worked with countless healthcare professionals over the years, and we've found the pressures and stresses of their day often put them in a similar time loop of feeling uncomfortable—of feeling not-OK. We have also found, through many long hours of observation, that patients are also stuck in a time loop of feeling not-OK about their medical situation. Why? Because they've come to expect a mediocre patient experience, visit after visit, medical office after medical office, year after year.

So let me ask you the questions I asked George: What if nothing changes? Will your healthcare professionals be able to maintain a profitable flow of patients, day after day? Will they be willing to adjust to the significant changes in the future of healthcare? Will they be supportive and cooperative with their peers? Will your patients be more understanding when their expectations are not met? Will they be more respectful of the professionals who care for them? Will they be raving about your medical practice?

Common sense and our own life experiences tell us the answer is, "No."

If nothing changes in the patient experience from how it is today, both staff and patients will be in a perpetual loop of feeling anxious, frustrated, and angry about their perceived experiences—which will affect the bottom line of the practice. If nothing changes for the healthcare professionals, they will continue feeling pressured, stressed, and defeated, day after

> *The patient experience is only as good as the internal culture of the practice.*

day—and these feelings will have a ripple effect on everyone with whom they come in contact.

Fortunately, there is a way out of the time loop. Sandler gives medical practices a low-stress, tried-and-true methodology to keep a profitable flow of patients coming through the practice who can't wait to tell others about the great experience they had.

After working with Sandler, Dr. George Upward was transformed. So was his practice. Whereas before he was worried about how to keep up with the "other guys," he now took the lead in his marketplace to set the standard for an extraordinary patient experience. For George and his team, the patient experience was an ongoing hot topic that permeated the whole practice. The hiring process changed to put a higher value on a person's customer-care skills. Champions of this culture enhancement were recognized and rewarded. Team huddles took place on a weekly basis to reinforce customer-care skills. Patients were surveyed on how they'd rate the patient experience, and the suggestions from these surveys were communicated to everyone. The sense of pride—from the frontline to the boardroom—was at its strongest. George had built a great medical practice.

Dr. Raina Rapport, MD, who had helped to found the practice, was much more comfortable setting the timeline for her retirement. She had emerged as "chief experience officer" for Upward Medicine—a title George saw fit to print right on her business card—and she became the primary role model for positive, peer-to-peer interactions. She spearheaded new ideas and best practices for working with others—best practices that expanded her own comfort zone. Her goal was to make her final year at Upward Medicine her best and to leave a legacy of which she could be proud. She was confident, finally, that both goals were in sight.

Ellen Everywhere, who spent most of her time at the front desk, found that, with George's support and coaching from Raina and Sandler, she could create a new reality for herself and her colleagues: a low-stress day at work. She had had no idea, just a few months prior, that such a reality was even possible.

Before I close this book, let me share with you the patient experience that lay at the heart of all three of these transformations.

WELCOME TO UPWARD MEDICINE

I want to take you to a very special place.

This is a place of healing and a place of business:

- A place that asks customers (patients) to invest their time and money in return for a service...
- A service that they will undoubtedly have to wait for, even though they've made an appointment...
- An appointment that is inconvenient and stressful because the customer anticipates being told bad news...
- News that will necessitate spending more time and money at this very same place.

Here's the kicker. This is a place that customers (patients) are now happy and willing to visit. That's how good the customer experience is.

Let's return to this place—to the new Upward Medicine—and take a closer look.

As you walk through the doors, you're met with the energy of a thriving office. Before the expected negatives—long wait, frustration, disrespect, stress—can take root in your head, you're greeted by a smiling Ellen Everywhere, who somehow finds you before you can make your way to the reception desk. She introduces herself, gets your name, and explains what you can expect during your visit. She is also ready to answer any questions that are on your mind. Ellen is happy to help you expedite that paperwork you were dreading, and she even takes care of checking you in. You never even make it up to the sliding glass window—and it turns out, you don't have to. Ellen is your concierge. You look around. The other patients don't seem frazzled. The room itself gives off a vibe that is more like a coffee shop than a waiting room.

The rest of your visit goes even better—much better than you expected, in fact. At each step of the visit, you were greeted with full attention and respect by a healthcare professional who approached you as a valued customer. That night, you post a note on Upward Medicine's social media page about how much you enjoyed interacting with Ellen and all the good people at the practice. You recommend Upward Medicine to family and friends.

HOW DID IT HAPPEN?

It happened because George, Raina, Ellen, and all the other members of the team at Upward Medicine were willing to move beyond their comfort zone—and a big part of that was being open to work with a Sandler trainer.

If you're ready to do the same, visit us at www.sandler.com/patient-care to continue the conversation.

> *And in the end, the love you take is equal to the love you make. —The Beatles*

Look for these other books
on shop.sandler.com:

Prospect the Sandler Way

Transforming Leaders the Sandler Way

Selling Professional Services the Sandler Way

Accountability the Sandler Way

Selling Technology the Sandler Way

LinkedIn the Sandler Way

Bootstrap Selling the Sandler Way

Customer Service the Sandler Way

Selling to Homeowners the Sandler Way

Succeed the Sandler Way

The Contrarian Salesperson

The Sales Coach's Playbook

Lead When You Dance

Change the Sandler Way

Motivational Management the Sandler Way

Call Center Success the Sandler Way

CONGRATULATIONS!

Patient Care the Sandler Way

includes a complimentary seminar!

Take this opportunity to personally experience the non-traditional sales training and reinforcement coaching that has been recognized internationally for decades.

Companies in the Fortune 1000 as well as thousands of small- to medium-sized businesses choose Sandler for sales, leadership, management, and a wealth of other skill-building programs. Now, it's your turn, and it's free!

You'll learn the latest practical, tactical, feet-in-the-street sales methods directly from your neighborhood Sandler trainers! They're knowledgeable, friendly, and informed about your local selling environment.

Here's how you redeem YOUR FREE SEMINAR invitation.

1. Go to www.Sandler.com and click on Find Training Location (top blue bar).
2. Select your location.
3. Review the list of all the Sandler trainers in your area.
4. Call your local Sandler trainer, mention *Patient Care the Sandler Way* and reserve your place at the next seminar!